Fired Up

not burnt out

Text copyright © Margaret Withers 2001
The author asserts the moral right
to be identified as the author of this work

Published by
The Bible Reading Fellowship
First Floor, Elsfield Hall
15–17 Elsfield Way, Oxford OX2 8FG
ISBN 1 84101 209 2

First published 2001
1 3 5 7 9 10 8 6 4 2 0
All rights reserved

Acknowledgments
Unless otherwise stated, scripture quotations are taken from the Good
News Bible published by The Bible Societies/HarperCollins Publishers Ltd,
UK © American Bible Society 1966, 1971, 1976, 1992,
used with permission.

Prayers starting 'Almighty God, we thank you for the gift…' copyright
© The Central Board of Finance of the Church of England, 1980;
The Archbishops' Council 1999, and 'Lord of the harvest…' copyright
© PCC St George's, Oakdale from *Patterns for Worship* (Church House
Publishing, 1995) reproduced by permission of the publishers.

Prayer from *Prayers for Children* (The National Society/Church House
Publishing, 1993) is copyright © Christopher Herbert and is reproduced
by permission of the publishers.

A catalogue record for this book is available from the British Library

Printed and bound in Great Britain by
Omnia Books Limited, Glasgow

Fired Up

not burnt out

EFFECTIVE CHILDREN'S LEADERSHIP FOR TODAY'S CHURCH

MARGARET WITHERS

Margaret Withers taught in several Inner London schools and for the Open University before becoming a Diocesan Children's Adviser in Rochester in 1989. She has spent the last decade heavily involved in providing training and support for voluntary children's leaders in parishes. In 1996, while Children's Officer for the diocese of Chelmsford, she established children's work as an integral part of Reader training as well as providing a similar input to several theological courses. The increasing demand for simple basic training for inexperienced leaders led to her writing a four-evening course for a group of parishes in 1998. This formed the basis of Fired up... not burnt out. *After a further two years in Rochester, she was appointed Archbishop's Officer for Evangelism among Children in June 2001. She is author of* Welcome to the Lord's Table *and* Toby and Trish and The Amazing Book of Acts, *both published under the Barnabas imprint.*

Thanks are due to:
The Revd Canon Penny Avann, and children's leaders from St John the Baptist, Beckenham, Kent; Mrs Mary Binks, Diocesan Children's Adviser, and children's leaders from the diocese of Blackburn, Lancashire; children's leaders from St Mary's Greenhithe, Kent and other local parishes, for piloting the course, and their many helpful comments.

FOREWORD

The religious experience of children is part of God's gift to them, theirs by nature and by grace. It is a gift not to them alone but to the whole Church, and the Church should receive and cherish the gift. Children themselves should recognize the value of the gift they receive and should learn to cherish it throughout their lives.

Their parents are ideally the first and best to help children recognize the gift, but others in the Church can help. Those who are called to work among children exercise a vital ministry—they are a great company—but too often they feel undervalued. They can become burnt out. Children's workers deserve recognition and resourcing through careful and thorough training. *Fired up... not burnt out* will make a significant contribution.

Margaret Withers brings knowledge, insight and depth to this book. It will greatly encourage those who work in the Church among children and equip them to reflect on the ministry to which they have been called. They should see themselves and their work as part of God's gracious gift.

Canon John Hall, General Secretary C of E Board of Education and General Secretary National Society (C of E) for Promoting Religious Education

'Helping a child to grow in faith and knowledge of God is one of the most precious gifts we can give to that young person.'

SECTION 1, UNIT A: WHAT DO I HAVE TO OFFER?

CONTENTS

Introduction

Fired up… not burnt out is designed to help people who find themselves working as volunteers with children in the church. It is in five sections, with two units in each section:

1. Called to communicate
   A. What do I have to offer?
   B. Tell the next generation

2. Using our senses
   A. Do you understand?
   B. Hidden treasures

3. Worship and spirituality
   A. An encounter with the living God
   B. Growing faith

4. The place of story
   A. The word of the Lord
   B. Mime, music and movement

5. Sharing and caring
   A. Reaching out
   B. Keeping safe

Postscript: The next step

Each unit includes the following:

- Aims of the unit: what we hope to achieve and discover.
- Introduction: information on the subject.
- Think or discuss: designed to help you to reflect on the material and move forward. This element may include practical activities, brainstorming, checklists and mini-research.

- Bible passage: summing up the unit with Jesus' teaching and other passages from scripture.
- Case study: thinking outside your own church—real situations for discussion.
- Prayer: used for preparation or for offering the completed unit to God.
- Further action: applying the things discussed in your own situation.
- Achievements: things you have learned.

This book is designed to help you to identify and use your gifts in working with children in the church. It provides the basic information that a new leader or helper needs. It also provides an opportunity for the experienced leader to review the present children's work in his or her church and to seek ways of developing it.

You can use the material in several different ways:

- As a structured programme led by an experienced mentor.
- A group of children's workers studying the book together, with members taking it in turn to lead a session.
- Reading the book under the guidance of an expert leader.
- Reading the book alone, but being prepared to ask questions of other people when they arise.
- As a reference book for clergy, authorized ministers or church council members.

Whichever way you use this book, the material is based on the premise that, because we are all different, we differ in our relationship with God and are at different places on our faith journeys. We have varied experiences of working with or knowing children, so we have a variety of perceptions and gifts to offer. We can enrich and be enriched by our companions as we talk about our faith, our ministry with children, and what we can bring to the work.

Whatever plan you are following, make it known to the people at your church that you are using this material. Ask them to pray for you and the children's work. If there are financial implications, do not hesitate to ask the church for funding. Our children's work belongs to the whole congregation and so deserves its support. Try to have your own copy of this book so that you can highlight points or jot comments in the margins. You will also want to refer back to it for information, as well as using the list of further reading and useful addresses (see Appendices B and C).

Preparation

If this material is used for training in a group, it is important to set aside some time to read each section or unit before the session. Rather than trying to absorb it all at once, concentrate first on the Bible passage and the prayer. These are the foundations of our relationship with God and the basis of our work with children. When you move on to the teaching and the case study, you are sure to find that there are thoughts and questions arising from them. Mark them with pencil or jot down your thoughts so that you can take them to the group.

At a group session

Remember that this is not a test on how much you know about children or what you have remembered about the unit! Rather, you are being invited to contribute your experience and thoughts.

You may find yourself working with people who have come from other traditions and situations from your own. Concentrate on listening and then contributing to what they have said. We can always learn from each other's experience. Naturally, there are basic rules of good practice, but there are very few totally right or wrong answers.

The most inexperienced leaders can often make a valuable contribution because they come to the work without much of the 'baggage' of past practice and history. If you are one of them, do not be afraid to speak out. Your contribution may be the one thing that nobody else has considered! If it is not, then you can learn from the ensuing discussion about it.

After the session, go through the 'Action and Achievement' sections. These should help you to put what you have learned into practice, and to review the aims of the unit in light of what you have learned.

Working alone

Two of the great strengths of attending a training course or studying a book in a group are sharing other people's experience and learning together. Studying alone can make the reader feel that everyone in the world knows far more on the subject than he or she does! If you are working alone, find a mentor with whom you can discuss the material. This could be an experienced leader, your vicar, minister, or a friend who works with children.

Try to set aside an uninterrupted hour each week for your study time. If this is not possible, divide each unit into two or three parts, preceding each one by reading through the Bible passage and prayer.

If you find that there are thoughts and questions arising from the teaching or the case study, mark them with pencil or jot them down. Arrange regular meetings with your mentor to discuss them. This is better than cornering your vicar on a Sunday morning or opening discussion in the middle of a supermarket queue. Speak openly with them about any questions that have arisen.

It is important that you should discuss the 'Action and Achievement' sections so that you can put into practice what you have learned, and also to recognize that you have taken on board the aims of the unit.

Whichever way you choose to work, allow God to become part of the time and space you have created for this study. He is the most important companion on your journey of discovery.

Leading a group

You may be a skilled teacher or trainer so you will be using this book as a framework to your own teaching. If your experience is of working in schools, remember that you will now be leading adults who have come from a variety of backgrounds and are there because they want to be. Part of your role is to impart information, but you will also be facilitating discussion, and you may well find that you gain as much from your group as you give to them.

If you are less experienced, do not worry. Each unit is set out with clear aims and questions for discussion, as well as a case study, so you have plenty of guidance. At the end of each unit, there are suggestions for helping with the major exercises but they are not the only or the best answers. You may find that the group comes up with better ones for its particular situation.

As this is a handbook as much as teaching material, it is designed so that you work on a whole section at each meeting. Do not spend time reading the material together. Ask the group to do that as part of their preparation. Then summarize the teaching in a couple of sentences and ask if there are any questions, before leading the discussion and exercises. For example, you might say, 'This unit starts with considering the ways that we learn. Apparently, we learn least by just listening and most by doing. Does anyone have any comments about that, or do you violently disagree? ... Yes, we do tend to say, "Sit still and listen" an awful lot—good point! ... So, let's look together at the exercise on the next page.'

Planning the programme

The material in this book can be presented in a variety of ways. Most children's workers are very busy people, so it can be difficult to find a pattern of meetings to suit even half a dozen leaders from the same congregation. Consider offering a combined course to several churches, maybe on a weekday evening, and then repeating it a few months later during the day. More people will be able to take part and it will allow for discussion between people of differing traditions and experience.

There are four different ways of organizing the programme:

- As a ten-session course, studying a unit at each meeting. Each unit is designed to last about an hour.
- In five sessions, studying a whole section at a time. This would ideally take place during the day so that a whole morning or afternoon could be used to cover both units and allow time for a break in between them.
- As a condensed course, lasting for five sessions of about 90 minutes, plus one practical workshop (see Appendix A).
- As a three- or four-day course, possibly held on several Saturdays or over a long weekend. This would need careful planning and adequate time for discussion and follow-up for the participants to get the full benefit of the course.

Preparing to lead a group

1. Include the sessions, the group members, and anything that you may find difficult or challenging in your personal prayers. Ask your vicar, minister or worship leader to remember the group in the intercessions at the Sunday worship.

2. Read the biblical passages. Each one connects with our work with children through referring to Jesus' teaching or other teaching within scripture. Let God speak to you through it and guide you in your understanding of the unit.

3. Look through the study outline for the meeting. Think about timing so that you don't let one part run on too long at the expense of another. Have a definite finishing time in mind. This should be about ten minutes before the end of the session to allow time for notices, information about the next session and the closing prayer. Note what points can be curtailed if time does run short.

4. Look at the questions and think about how the discussion might go. Be prepared for it to take a different line, but do not lose sight of the aims at the beginning of the unit. Close any discussion by drawing together the main points and then asking if there is anything that you have forgotten or that needs to be added. This will give people a chance to review the discussion, or make notes, while allowing everyone to feel that their contribution has been heard.

5. Prepare the meeting place in advance. Think about the arrangement of chairs, remembering that people may need to work in pairs or groups but that they should be able to see each other's faces. When working as a whole group, a circle or horseshoe is usually best.

6. See that any resources and equipment are nearby. You do not need any elaborate resources, but large sheets of paper and felt-tipped pens are useful. You will probably want to use other resources such as craft materials, or taped music in Section 4B, 'Music, mime and movement'.

7. The ideal size of a group for this type of training is between six and ten people. This allows variety and discussion. If you have many more people, you have to adopt a more formal approach. Feedback from discussion will also take a long time, so consider splitting a large group into two if possible.

When the group meets

1. Arrive early so that you can greet everyone.
2. At the first session, get members to introduce themselves to each other.
3. Arrange to share any tasks like making coffee or provision of equipment as appropriate.
4. Try to include everyone in discussion by saying things like, 'You are looking thoughtful. What do you want to add?' Be firm but polite with the person who is inclined to take over, by identifying and inviting other people to speak first.
5. Do not talk too much yourself. Allow time for silence and thought. If discussion seems to be getting nowhere, draw together the subjects that have been raised, then ask if there is anything else to be added.
6. Always include worship at the beginning or end. See that it is of the same standard as the rest of the session.
7. As time goes on, you will identify people who have expertise in various subjects. Encourage them to lead part of a session. Encourage everyone to get involved in leading the worship and other appropriate sections as part of their training.

After a session

1. Think through the session. Note anything that was good and encouraging about it. Then think about anything that went wrong or could have been done better. See if you have any ideas about how to do it better next time.
2. Make written notes to remind yourself what needs to be done before the next session.
3. Be aware of your mistakes, and address them, rather than hoping that they will automatically be put right next time.

CALLED TO COMMUNICATE

UNIT A:
WHAT DO I HAVE TO OFFER?

Aims of the unit
- To explore our reasons for working with children.
- To recognize that each one of us has qualities and skills to offer.
- To examine the support available for children's work and its leaders.

Bible passage: 1 Corinthians 12:27–28

Introduction: Making Christ known

Helping a child to grow in faith and knowledge of God is one of the most precious gifts we can give to that young person. You may have decided to work with children in your church because you have a longing to do just that and have found that you have a talent for communicating with young people. If that is so, it is wonderful. Many people, however, would say that they are doing it for another reason as well, or even more than one. Here are some of the most common ones:

1. There is a shortage of leaders, so you were asked to help on two Sundays each month.
2. You feel that the present children's work is poor and that you could do something to improve it.
3. You have young children of your own and want to provide something on Sundays for them and their friends.
4. You helped with a fun morning and found that you enjoyed it. Now the parish wants to start a mid-week club and is looking for a leader.
5. Your church services are so awful that you would rather be with the children.

6. Your daily work is with children, so you feel that you should get involved in the holiday club.
7. The minister said that there was nobody else!

Responding to need

None of these reasons sound like a dramatic call from God to carry out his work, but we often do things for all sorts of reasons and only discern God's hand in our decisions when we look back. The first four reasons show that you have seen a need and filled it. That is responding to a clear demand. Whatever the reason, you will need help and support. Even the most experienced of workers can always learn new ideas. If you want to improve the present work or are joining an established team, you will need to ensure you use moderation and tact with the other leaders.

It is amazing how many children's leaders admit to number 5 and only come to church when they are working with the children. Others come with feelings that they ought to be involved in children's work because they are working with children professionally. Still others offer to help because nobody else is willing to be involved. If this is the case, you are still responding to God's call to do this valuable work, but you will need to have support for your own spiritual life if the children are to grow in faith without your becoming drained of energy and ideas. This is discussed further in section 3B, 'Growing Faith'.

Bible reading

Read Paul's description of the Christian community as being like a body made up of many parts.

> All of you are Christ's body, and each one is a part of it. In the church God has put all in place: in the first place apostles, in the second place prophets, and in the third place teachers; then those who perform miracles, followed by those who are given the power to heal or to help others or to direct them or to speak in strange tongues.

1 CORINTHIANS 12:27–28

In his letters, Paul uses the term 'body' in two ways. He often describes Christians as being Christ's body on earth, his Church. Here, he uses the term to describe a group of members who work together for the common good of the community. It may seem that the gift of teaching is the prime skill needed in children's work but this is not the whole picture. Other gifts are of equal importance and may be your main reason for getting involved: for example, Paul specifically mentioned those of carer, friend, support and guide. You may have other gifts and experience to offer. Maybe you are good at craft or acting, or have training in first aid. If you are a parent, you will probably be used to telling stories, answering questions simply, and responding to children's needs. All of these gifts and many more can be used to build up a balanced team of children's workers. Your diocese, denomination and various organizations offer training to help you to develop particular skills.

Think or discuss

Using your time and talents in children's work
You may be working with an established group, or you might feel that you have a ministry with children but do not know how to address it. Take a little time to think about what time and talents you have to offer and how they match with the needs of your church and wider community.

- What are my real reasons for doing this work?
- What time do I have available?
- Do I need an opt-out clause if things are not working out?
- What gifts and experience can I bring to this work?
- What are the needs of the children in my church and community?
- Are there any talents that another member of the group has that he or she has not mentioned?
- What training or other opportunities to increase my gifts and skills are available?

Taking each point in turn, think of or discuss your honest answer to each question. Note anything that occurs to you for the first time or surprises you. Is there anything you can do now besides reading this book to equip your ministry with children? A checklist to help you to explore the various types of children's work is at the end of this unit.

Help and support

Although you may have worked on this unit as a group, the focal point has been you as an individual, your reasons for doing this work, and the time and talents you have to offer. If you are reading this at home on your own, you may find all sorts of questions that you want to ask someone. Children's and youth leaders often feel very isolated and under-valued so it is important that you start any training by exploring the help and support you should have from your congregation, fellow leaders, and the wider Church.

Responsibilities and relationships

Anything that takes place in the name of the church is the legal responsibility of the priest or minister and the church council. They should have agreed that you may work with children and, if you are new to this work, you should have signed a criminal declaration form. This gives some basic information about you and includes permission for a police check. This may appear rather onerous but it is there to protect you as well as the children. You know that the church council has authorized you to do this work and, if something ever goes wrong, you will have its support. That should give you confidence in what you are doing. In exchange, you should regularly inform the church council about your work and keep to basic health and safety standards. These are discussed in section 5B, 'Keeping safe'.

It is a good idea to have some kind of written agreement, or job description, so that you know what your responsibilities are and to whom you should refer when changes are necessary or difficulties arise. Most problems arise with voluntary work because people do not know what is expected of them or the correct forum for discussion. Your priest or minister should give you support by taking an interest in your planning meetings and by being available should you have a concern that you wish to discuss. If you have a paid children's or youth worker, they should attend your meetings and be prepared to offer advice and training. Some churches have an education committee that plans all of the adult and children's nurture. The children's and youth work should be prayed for regularly in the Sunday intercessions.

The way that children are valued and leaders affirmed largely depends on the attitude of the clergy and church council. Children have no voice, so it is important to see that their interests are represented. You can do this in several ways.

- Vote for people to be on your church council who will support the work with children and young people. This includes seeing that proper health and safety standards are maintained.
- See that people who are working with children and young people are represented on committees concerned with worship, education, and social events.
- Have a budget for children's work that includes funds for leaders' training and resources. This puts the work into the accounts that are presented at the Annual General Meeting.
- Present reports on all the children's work at the AGM and use the church magazine to keep the congregation informed.
- Ask the parish to remember the children's work in its prayers.

Taking each point in turn, think or discuss whether the church council gives you and your work the support you need.

Case study: Sara's Sundays

Sara has two sons, Ben (9) and Charles (6), who attend the local church primary school. She started going to church through attending school services, and goes about once a fortnight. She enjoys hearing Ben sing in the choir while Charles goes to the Sunday Club. Gary, Sara's husband, is not interested in the church at all. He is assistant manager of a supermarket. Sara used to be a nurse but now works part-time supporting a disabled teenage girl in a secondary school. She has been asked to help with Sunday Club for two Sundays each month.

- What experience and gifts will Sara bring to the Sunday Club?
- How could Sara's working in the Sunday Club affect Ben, Charles and Gary?
- How do you suggest that Sara spends Sunday mornings when she is not helping with Sunday Club?
- What support will Sara need if she is to develop her own faith?

Further action

- Work out your strategy for studying this book. This may involve organizing a babysitter, having supper early or setting aside an hour at a regular time.
- Think about what you have to offer to the children's work in your church. Stay aware that God may be calling you to do something different as a result of this study.
- Think about your own spiritual life. If you are now involved in working with children on Sundays, see that you get a regular Sunday off or can attend a mid-week service. You also need to set aside time for your own prayer and Bible reading. There is more information on this in Unit 3A, 'An encounter with the living God'.
- Remember that you need to spend time with your family and friends, especially if they do not attend church with you.

Prayer

Remember, O Lord, what you have wrought in us and not what we deserve. But, as you have called us to your service, make us worthy of our calling; through Jesus Christ our Lord.

BOOK OF COMMON PRAYER, 1928

❖

Achievements

You should now be able to:

- Discern the reasons for your doing this work.
- Know the qualities and skills that you are already bringing to it.
- Start considering the most effective ways of using your time and talents to fulfil the needs of the children while not neglecting your own spiritual life.
- Know the legal and other support that you should expect and some ways of getting it.
- Identify areas where you may benefit from further training.

USING YOUR TIME AND TALENTS IN CHILDREN'S WORK: A PERSONAL CHECKLIST

Time

Being involved during Sunday worship

- Does your Junior Church need regular help or someone who would fill in occasionally when a leader needs a free Sunday?
- Are there some mothers with toddlers who need someone to help them, either by sitting with them in the pew or in a crèche area?
- Could you help to prepare or take part in the Family Service?

Being involved during the daytime or early evenings

- Do you have a pre-school or parent-and-toddler club that needs helpers, or is there a need for one? The local Early Years and Child-care Partnership will provide advice. This may include training and financial support if the club is registered with it. Contact your Early Years' Development officer. The Pre-school Learning Alliance will also provide advice.
- Could you get involved in starting or helping in a midweek club where children have activities that include some Christian teaching? Contact your local Childcare Partnership officer as above. Kids' Club Network will also provide advice and training.
- Uniformed organizations, youth groups and sporting or drama clubs always need helpers. Contact the local group leader.

Being involved at special events or on specific occasions

- Many children receive their only Christian teaching through a holiday club or a 'fun day'. A large number of adults are needed for a short time, both working with the children and providing publicity, making coffee and doing other odd jobs.

- A child who is being prepared for baptism, holy communion or confirmation may need support, ranging from sponsorship and practical help to escorting him or her to classes.

Talents

Craft

Could you use or teach your particular craft as part of a session of the Junior Church or club? Seasonal cooking like hot cross buns is popular; so are crafts that link with a scriptural subject.

Drama and dancing

Could you organize a short drama for the Family Service or an entertainment for a parish social event? Could you involve the youth group in some acting?

Music

Many youngsters play musical instruments. If there is a group, could you support it by playing in it or working with some youngsters to play occasionally in church? Could you teach new hymns or songs to the Junior Church?

Bell-ringing

Many church bells are silent for lack of ringers, yet about 11,000 of England's bell-ringers are under 17. Could you get back into practice and help other youngsters?

Sport

Could you run a five-a-side football team or organize occasional sports' afternoons?

If these questions have made you rethink the ways that you could use your time and talents to help in children's work, take time to think it through and pray about it. We will be discussing this further in Units 4B and 5A.

UNIT B:
TELL THE NEXT GENERATION

Aims of the unit
- To examine the importance of children's work.
- To explore the aims and priorities of the work.
- To become aware of common misconceptions and pitfalls.

Bible passage: Psalm 78:1–7

Introduction: Why should we have children's work?

'What a silly question!' you think, but is it easy to give an answer? 'Well, we have always had children's work' or 'We have to do something for the children' are common replies. Before we explore the question further, let's look briefly at the history of the most well-known form of children's work in the Church, the Sunday school.

To teach children to read and observe the sabbath

Robert Raikes opened the first well-known Sunday school in 1780 in the Sooty Alley area of Gloucester. Children, who worked in the factories and mills, spent their Sundays running wild through the streets. Raikes started the school to teach them to read and to keep them out of mischief. His work in the local prison had given him a vivid picture of the way that ignorance bred crime. He became convinced that the best way to cure crime was to deal with the underlying cause.

Similar classes sprang up all over the country. Their aim was to teach children to read the Bible and behave properly on the sabbath. Attempts to expand the children's education with classes in writing and arithmetic were often questioned. These were not appropriate subjects for the Sabbath, a day of leisure! But the fire had been kindled. Some Sunday schools became evening classes, with lending libraries and clothing clubs attached. Others eventually became day schools.

To teach the faith to the fringe

Whatever the original aims of these pioneers, the ideal of free education for the poor sprang from these roots. When schooling became compulsory, Sunday schools did not close down. They turned their attention to providing basic Christian teaching for children, mostly those who did not come to church. A national pattern of teaching developed, supported by the Sunday School Union, the National Society and other organizations. Training courses, certificates and education councils were established. And so it remained until after World War II. But the world was changing fast. By the last quarter of the 20th century, most non-church parents had stopped sending their children to Sunday school.

To nurture Christian children

Yet again, the Sunday schools changed. Teachers turned their attention to the children of the congregation. Sessions ran at the same time as the morning service, the children often joining the adults for part of it. Monthly Family Services or 'all-age worship' with visual aids, drama and lively music were designed to provide accessible worship for young people and the increasing numbers of adults who had little knowledge of the Christian faith. And that is the most common pattern today.

What about the outsiders?

But what has happened to our ministry with the vast numbers of children who have had no Christian education at all?

Many churches have little outreach to these youngsters. Others organize holiday clubs, fun mornings and midweek clubs, geared towards children who have no other links with the church. Some of these youngsters may then turn up for the occasional special service, although most will not become part of the main worshipping community. But the seeds of the Christian faith have been sown, however thinly. We can only hope and pray that at some time in the future, they will bear fruit. We will be looking at ways of reaching non-church children in Unit 5A.

At the beginning of the 21st century, after so many changes, it is not surprising that the question, 'Why should we have children's work' is difficult to answer. With so many new demands, how can churches decide where their priorities lie and how can the workers evaluate what they are doing?

Think or discuss

Aims of children's work

Here are some of the most common reasons given for having children's work. Write each one on a strip of paper. On your own, or in pairs or threes, try to arrange the strips in some sort of order of priority. This will probably not be a straight line. You may want to make three clusters: good, middling and bad reasons. Alternatively, you can make a list with 'wings' if some reasons seem to belong together.

1. For the children to be looked after while the adults worship.
2. To teach the children about God in a way that they understand.
3. To encourage the parents to come to church.
4. To ensure the future of your church.
5. To give the children a happy time.
6. To teach the children Bible stories.
7. To teach moral and social behaviour.
8. To help Christian parents to bring up their children in the Christian faith.
9. To reach out to children who have no knowledge of the Christian faith.
10. For children to experience belonging to a Christian community.
11. To give children an experience of worshipping God.
12. For children to become friends and followers of Jesus.

Your first reaction is probably that none of the statements gives a complete answer.

- Are there any that you wish to discard completely?
- Talk through the reasons for the way you have arranged your list with the other people in your group or your mentor.
- Is there anything that you now want to alter?

Some comments to help your discussion are at the end of this unit.

Bible reading

Here is the psalmist's answer to the question, 'Why should we have children's work?'

> Listen, my people, to my teaching, and pay attention to what I say. I am going to use wise sayings and explain mysteries from the past, things we have heard and known, things that our ancestors told us. We will not keep them from our children; we will tell the next generation about the Lord's power and his great deeds and the wonderful things he has done. He gave laws to the people of Israel and commandments to the descendants of Jacob. He instructed our ancestors to teach his laws to their children, so that the next generation might learn them and in turn should tell their children. In this way they also would put their trust in God and not forget what he has done, but always obey his commandments.
>
> PSALM 78:1–7

The message in the psalm is clear. We are to tell our children the story of God's saving work among us.

Think or discuss

People living in the Middle East thousands of years ago wrote the Bible. We live in Western Europe in the 21st century, so it can appear very remote. Some parts of it may even seem immoral. Elements of our worship may also seem strange. Do we take trouble to explain these 'mysteries' so that the children can relate to them and thus hear God's word?

The tradition was for the father of the family to hand on the story to his children. What should we be doing to support parents in this role? In our support, are we sensitive to the special needs of single parents and stepfamilies? What place does reaching out to children from non-church families have in our children's and youth work?

Are there things in our church that prevent children hearing the story? Look back at the decisions made by your church council during the past year. Did they help young families to be part of the Christian community or did they hinder them?

Do we celebrate our faith and trust in God? Do we let his goodness to us show in our lives?

Do we help children to apply God's commandments to their daily lives?

What goes on in my church?

Take a piece of paper and red, blue and yellow pens or three highlighter pens. Make a list of everything that happens in your church community, services, social events, clubs and other activities.

Write a 'C' against all the ones that involve children.

Now mark those that are part of their spiritual lives in red, those that are social events in blue, and those that use skills and gifts in yellow. Note that some of them will use two or maybe all three colours. For example, playing in a music group is concerned with worship and musical skill, and has a social aspect.

There should be a spread of all three colours. Are there obvious things that are lacking? Are there events where children and adults come together? Compare your results and see where you can use ideas from other churches.

Case study: Why are you out there?

St Mary's is the principal church in a town of 30,000 people. It is in an area of high deprivation and the congregation is small and elderly. Since the curate arrived, there has been a sudden influx of children.

The Junior Church previously numbered six; now it has nearly forty youngsters. Several people are willing to help but nobody will lead the teaching, so the vicar and curate take turns. Several of the congregation have grumbled. 'Why are you out there with them? The priests should be in church, leading the worship.' The clergy have responded that they are doing it because nobody from the congregation has come forward.

- Who is responsible for the care and nurture of our children?
- Can you think of a way that this situation could be used to teach about children being part of the church?
- Can you think of any ways of easing this situation?
- Does your priest or minister visit your children's group? Does he or she ever take an active part in their nurture?

Although aspects of it may be delegated to you, our children's nurture is the responsibility of the whole Christian community. Children will learn most about worshipping God from the way that the congregation worships him. They will learn about how God regards children from the way that Christians, especially church leaders, behave towards them. They will learn how Christians should behave from the way that the adult Christians behave towards them.

Further action

Be aware, and make it clear to others, that the children's nurture is the responsibility of the whole congregation.

- Think about the example you set towards the children. Can you improve it?
- Invite your priest or minister to visit your children's group.
- Consider if any members of the congregation can be involved within a session.
- Note where there are gaps in the provision for children and consider if just one of them could be filled in easily.

❖

Prayer

Christ has no body now on earth but yours,
No hands but yours, no feet but yours;
Yours are the eyes
Through which to look at Christ's compassion to the world,
Yours are the feet
With which he is to go about doing good,
And yours are the hands
With which he is to bless us now.

Teresa of Avila (1515–82)

❖

Achievements

You should now be able to:
- Know the aims and priorities of your children's work.
- Keep them in mind when talking about them or making any plans or decisions.
- Make the importance of children's work known to your church leaders and congregation and ask for their support.
- Identify areas where improvements need to be made.

Comments on the 'Aims of children's work' exercise

There are no perfect answers to this exercise but the aims can be put into four clusters. Some could belong in more than one cluster or be grouped quite differently. You may totally disagree with these comments and that is fine!

1. Knowing God (2, 6 and 11)

We have children's work in order that children can worship God and learn about him in a way that is appropriate for their age and experience (2 and 11).

This will always involve Bible stories, especially ones about the life, death and resurrection of Jesus. They need to be applied to everyday situations and linked with worship (6 and 11) as well as the aims in the second cluster.

2. I belong: come and join us (9, 10 and 12)

We express part of our relationship with God by belonging to a Christian community. This is not just your church club or your parish. It is the great company of Christians all over the world, with those who have died and are now in heaven. Children need to be made welcome as part of the Christian family (10). A Christian is a follower of Jesus Christ. Part of our work is about making new disciples, both children and adults (12).

If we value our faith and want children to learn about it, experience belonging to the Church and become disciples of Jesus Christ, then surely, outreach to both children and adults is vital (9). A static church is a dying church! Let us look at this aim more closely.

In our outreach, what do we want to happen? Is outreach about giving children a chance to hear and respond to the gospel? Or is it really about increasing our congregation? Can we accept that we are sowing seeds of faith but may never see the harvest? On the other hand, can we give anything but the highest priority to proclaiming the gospel to people who might go through their lives without hearing it?

3. Outcomes of the aims (3, 4, 7 and 8)

Being a Christian makes certain demands on our lives, including the way we behave, and giving up time to worship God. This includes supporting parents (8) and social and moral teaching (7), as well as welcoming whole families and building the Church of the future (3 and 4). These are outcomes rather than aims in themselves.

❖

4. Hidden benefits (1 and 5)

This leaves two aims. Some people will discard them, saying that if they are the aims, we might as well buy the children some chips and sit them in front of a video. But before we consign these aims to the bin, let us look at them again.

If your work takes place on Sunday, you are occupying the children while their parents worship (1). Some of your congregation will see this as being principally child-minding. You need to make it clear that overcrowding, or including toddlers because their parents need a break, is not an option. Go back to the first cluster and read the Bible passage to remind yourself of the underlying aims and responsibilities of this work. Then ensure that you have adequate facilities to meet the needs of the children and their leaders.

Do not worry about making your children happy (5). If your work is carefully prepared and well resourced, and if the children are welcomed as valued members of the Christian community and come to know the living God, the result will be true happiness beyond anything that you can provide.

USING OUR SENSES

Unit A:
Do you understand?

Aims of the unit
- To explore ways in which we learn.
- To investigate appropriate methods of teaching.
- To consider effective ways of using space and time.

Bible passage: John 13:4–9, 12–14

Introduction: Helping children to learn

We often start to plan a session by deciding what we want to teach. That may not be more detailed than noting the subject of the Bible passage. We tell the children about Elijah or about the sower, and then they do an activity. The children may have had an enjoyable time, but what have they learned about God's relationship with his people? Has it helped them to have a relationship with him? Was it the same as what you intended to teach?

A book of this size cannot claim to provide a full guide to child development and teaching techniques, and it is not necessary for a leader to be an expert on them. But how can we help our children not just to learn a number of Bible stories, but to understand them as the story of God's saving work and to apply them to their daily lives? How can we help them to worship God the creator and come to have a relationship with Jesus, their friend and brother?

Come and see

Think about a remote part of the world, Antarctica. How do you know that it exists? What makes it real and exciting to you?

- Hearing a talk on the radio about it?
- Reading about it?
- Seeing a television programme about it?
- Seeing a video and then writing about it?
- Going there yourself?

We learn from every one of the above methods, but we gain and remember the least from just listening, and the most from doing. Writing or drawing a picture will strengthen the knowledge gained from seeing a video or reading a story. 'Going there' (i.e., doing something) is usually the best way, but it is not always practical. It is often too expensive or takes too long. In our teaching, we need a mixture of activities where we combine the things that have been heard and seen with practical activities of various kinds.

The five senses of sight, hearing, touch, taste and smell are the tools by which we learn. Add movement to the list and we have the ingredients for effective learning. Sight is the most powerful way of taking in and memorizing facts. Listening on its own is not a very effective way of learning. The phrase 'in one ear and out the other' bears grains of truth. We remember the things that we do for longer than those that we hear. We learn more from what we do than from what we observe. Many behaviour problems, or complaints that church services are 'boring', stem from people being expected to sit still and listen for long periods of a time. Eyes flicker around for some diversion and the mind begins to wander. The need to translate this into action is greater in children than adults. A toddler will head off down the church to be closer to the action, providing the older congregation with a welcome distraction.

There are occasions when a very motivated child will become completely immersed in an activity, but generally, children have only short attention spans and constantly need fresh approaches to help them to learn.

Listening to a story and colouring in a picture is the norm far too often. Craft, drama, music, games, finding things in the church and churchyard, cooking and eating are all vital components of a good session.

❖

Activities

Use your senses

Take five large sheets of paper. Head them: Sight, Hearing, Touch, Movement, Smell/Taste. Make checklists of the methods and activities that we can use in our work that use each sense. If you are working with a group, divide into five pairs and give each one a particular checklist to complete. After a few minutes, invite each pair to read out their list in turn and invite the other participants to add their own ideas to it. Alternatively, pin the sheets up around the room and invite the participants to walk around and contribute to them as they get ideas.

Specimen checklists are given at the end of this unit.

- Think back to a recent session with the children. Did it have a balance between using all the senses or was it almost entirely through sight and sound?
- How much of the session involved sitting still and listening?
- Are there any ways in which you could have improved on it by altering just one or two things?

Find a space and move in it

The way that you make use of your space can have a big effect on the way the children learn as well as the way you teach. It also affects their behaviour and attitude to the sessions. This is discussed in Unit 5B, 'Keeping safe'.

If you are working in a hall, divide it into areas for the various activities. Have a worship area in which a table is set up with a cross or an open Bible, flowers or candles. Assign an open space for games and drama, another area for storytelling and music, and have tables for art and craft set up in a separate space. See that you use each area at some time in the session. This provides a strong framework, which gives security, as well as encouraging the children to move about. If you need guidance with planning, visit a local pre-school that operates in a hall to see how it is laid out.

If you are in a small room, sit around a mat or at a table. Place a candle in the centre as a focal point for the worship. Encourage the children to move within the limited space by standing for the prayers, sharing the Peace, and sitting for the story. Make a 'Ready Box', a crate which contains items like pens, paper, scissors and glue, which keeps the area tidy and can be produced at the appropriate time. If possible, use small stackable tables for crafts and set them up in their own area.

Make full use of the church building and churchyard. Information on tombstones can sometimes be used in teaching, but always remind the children to treat graves with respect. Utilize the space in the church by letting the children take up their collection bag, show and talk about their activities, and display their art and crafts.

Children of a wide age-range meeting in the same room presents a problem in itself. If possible, assign a separate space for the oldest group, even if it is only a ring of chairs in a lobby. Encourage them to be involved in the main worship by singing, serving, reading or assisting the welcomers. It might be appropriate to encourage them to come to a church service regularly and then to have their nurture on occasional Saturday or Sunday evenings, or as part of an activity morning.

Bible reading

This is an account of one of Jesus' most effective pieces of teaching. Read it through, then take it a line or two at a time and think about the teaching techniques that Jesus used to get across his message.

Jesus rose from the table, took off his outer garment, and tied a towel round his waist. Then he poured some water into a basin and began to wash the disciples' feet and dry them with the towel round his waist. He came to Simon Peter, who said to him, 'Are you going to wash my feet, Lord?'

Jesus answered him, 'You do not understand now what I am doing, but you will understand later.'

Peter declared, 'Never at any time will you wash my feet!'

'If I do not wash your feet,' Jesus answered, 'you will no longer be my disciple.'

Simon Peter answered, 'Lord, do not wash only my feet then! Wash my hands and head, too!' ...

After Jesus had washed their feet, he put his outer garment back on and returned to his place at the table. 'Do you understand what I have just done to you?' he asked. 'You call me Teacher and Lord, and it is right that you do so, for that is what I am. I, your Lord and Teacher, have just washed your feet. You, then, should wash one another's feet.'

JOHN 13:4–9, 12–14

Think or discuss

- The disciples had met together for the Passover meal. It was a celebration between friends. What did Jesus do to get their attention?
- Think through the actual act of foot-washing. What senses are being used?
- How did Jesus respond to Simon Peter's question, 'Are you going to wash my feet, Lord?' What did Peter learn from the conversation? How do you respond to the apparently unnecessary question?
- What did Jesus want the disciples to learn from the action?
- What made this example of Jesus' teaching so powerful?
- Think or discuss how you could use this as a model for your teaching.

Case study: Starting and stopping

The famous musician Sir Thomas Beecham was supposed to have said to an orchestra, 'Start together. Finish together. Then the audience will be content with what happens in between.' First impressions are vital. They are the ones that catch the attention and set the tone of the session. The last moment is the one the participants take away with them.

Rose started the story of Noah's Ark by saying, 'One day, lots of people had been very naughty, and God got really angry with them.'

At the end of the story, Robin asked, 'Does God still drown people who are naughty?'

- What would you want the children to learn about God from the Noah story?
- Remembering that first impressions catch the listener's attention, how would you have started the story?
- What would you have used as a visual aid? Notice how the focus of the story changes according to the different visual aids members of the group have chosen.
- How do you deal with questions about illness, death and natural disasters?
- Why is the Noah story seen to be especially suitable for children? Is the message behind it really an easy one for children to understand?

Make sure that your sessions have a summing-up time. Sit everyone down for a few seconds and go through together what you have learned. Don't confine it to the title of the story and the things you did, but include what you have found out about God and his people, or about being a Christian. Include reminders about the previous weeks in the next session so that you are constantly reinforcing the basic information and building on it.

Further action

- Think what you aim for the children to learn. Consider this when deciding how to start and finish your session.
- Use the 'senses' exercise in your preparation of future sessions. Aim to have something from at least three columns in every session that you do.
- Review the way that your space is used. Consider especially the needs of the oldest group.

❖

Prayer
O gracious and holy Father,
give us wisdom to perceive you,
intelligence to understand you,
diligence to seek you,
patience to wait for you,
eyes to behold you,
a heart to meditate on you,
and a life to proclaim you
through the power of the spirit of Jesus Christ our Lord.
ATTRIBUTED TO BENEDICT (480–543)

❖

Achievements
You should now be able to:
- Have some understanding of how children learn.
- Utilize the children's senses and find effective ways of starting and closing sessions.
- Identify ways of using your surroundings to help the children to learn and feel secure.

A CHECKLIST FOR THE EXERCISE ON USING YOUR SENSES

Here are some of the most common ways that we can use our senses in teaching our children. You will probably think of others. Notice that some of them, like drama, go across several senses. Also, note that some are strongly connected with worship. We worship God with all of ourselves. This should involve using all of our senses to a greater or lesser degree.

Sight	Hearing	Touch	Movement	Taste/Smell
Books	Speaking	Craft	Drama	Cooking
Pictures/posters	Singing	Model making	Dance	Meals and parties
OHP	Listening	Painting	Team games	Flowers
Drama	Stories	Collage	Parachute	Incense and
Church building	Drama	The Peace	games	scented candles
and furnishings	Musical	Drama	Posture and	
Churchyard	instruments	Ring games	gesture	
Candles	Tapes and CDs	Cooking	Churchyard and	
Videos		Feeling objects	other visits	
Computer			Processions	
Worksheets				

UNIT B:
HIDDEN TREASURES

Aims of the unit

- To examine ways in which the church building is a powerful teaching aid.
- To explore and appreciate the gift of the Christian year.
- To touch upon using signs, symbols, talents and experiences to reveal some of God's glory.

Bible passage: John 2:1–11

Introduction: Let the building speak

We have used the previous unit to look at ways in which we teach and learn effectively, by using our senses, being clear about our aims and knowing the techniques which help people to retain information. Look back at the checklist of ways that we can use our senses to help us to learn. Some of the most powerful ones, like processions, the Peace, candles, incense and flowers are used in worship, though we can still include them in our teaching.

Churches are most wonderful teaching aids, but we tend to neglect this by only looking at them from an historical perspective. Many congregations tend to see their church building as an expensive and confining burden, and few, if any, are child-friendly. Others may think that because their building is simple or they worship in a hall, it cannot be a teaching aid. However, even the simplest of church buildings has features that we can use in helping children to learn about their faith. They include:

- Shape, size, and style of the building.
- Stained-glass windows, pictures and icons.

- Symbols and designs on furnishings.
- Font or baptistry, pulpit, altar or communion table.
- Use of colours and lights.
- Books.
- Musical instruments.

Learning on foot

Go for a walk around your church. It may not be very attractive, but the sense of God's presence will have been created there by the architecture, decorations and furnishing, whatever its style and age. Think about what the position and size of a cross, an open Bible, the altar table, or the height of the pulpit says to us and to our children.

Stained-glass windows and murals taught the faith to generations of people who could not read. Today's children use television and the Internet for much of their education and read books far less. We need to respond to this trend by recovering the use of visual images. Look at the windows and pictures. Note the people who are portrayed there, what stories they tell, and anything else about them that could be a useful teaching aid. Search for symbols in carvings and furnishings. Showing a kneeler with St Peter's keys, or a dove to symbolize the Holy Spirit, may seize the children's attention at the beginning of a story, and then lead to a treasure hunt for symbols in the building.

The font or baptistry is an enormous teaching aid. Most of your children will have seen someone being baptized. Some may remember or be looking forward to their own baptism. Think what message its position in the building, either by the door or in the centre of the building, gives to us. The shape is also symbolical: roundness reminds us of the eternity of God; an octagon shows the seven days of the creation, with the eighth side being the resurrection, our new creation. A rectangle is the shape of a grave; in baptism we are buried and then risen with Christ.

A candle reminds us that Jesus is the light of the world. Candles are being increasingly rediscovered, used at baptisms and Easter, when the Gospel is read and as an aid to prayer. Note how candles are used in your church. Think of ways in which you could use them in your teaching.

What shall we do today?

The changing pattern of the Church's year is another gift that we tend to neglect. Much schoolwork revolves around seasons and moods, festivals and holidays, while celebrations like birthdays and Christmas are major events in a child's year. The Christian calendar covers all experiences of life. Many churches now use a Lectionary, a programme of prayers and readings, based on a three-year cycle that also covers a large amount of scripture. Refer back to the 'Aims' exercise in Unit 1B. Here we saw that the Bible needs to be connected to our relationship with God and our daily life, not just taught as historical stories.

Think or discuss

Many churches use different colours according to the days and seasons. Remember that seeing is a far more effective way of learning than just being told something. Colour, smell and movement are powerful teaching tools. Lists of the liturgical colours and commonly used symbols are at the end of this unit.

Think about the appearance of your church on Good Friday. What words and feelings spring to mind? Now think about how it looks and feels, even smells, on Easter morning. How does it make you feel? What colours are predominant? Even a complete stranger can sense the story in the atmosphere and surroundings, and that will give more strength to the direct teaching in lessons and sermons.

Brainstorm

Together or in small groups, list five key words or phrases connected with each season or festival of the Church's year.

1. Advent
2. Christmas
3. Epiphany
4. Candlemas
5. Lent

6. Holy Week
7. Easter and Ascension
8. Pentecost
9. Harvest Thanksgiving
10. All Saints' tide

Now add an object or symbol that can be used to illustrate each season. Collect up your answers. You should have enough visual aids and topics to keep you going for some time.

Lectionary-based material

There are now several children's teaching courses that are based on the Church's year and three-year cycle of readings. Apart from the above points, it has the advantage that the Old Testament and Gospel readings are semi-continuous, so they allow everyone to follow a particular story or theme. It also provides continuity between weeks when the children are in or not in church and strengthens links between the main service and the children's worship.

Bible reading

Before reading the account of Jesus' first miracle, make an attractive setting that appeals to the senses. Put a lighted candle, or flowers and a cross, on a coloured cloth. Include two glasses, one filled with water, the other with wine.

> There was a wedding in the town of Cana in Galilee. Jesus' mother was there, and Jesus and his disciples had also been invited to the wedding. When the wine had given out, Jesus' mother said to him, 'They have no wine left.'
>
> 'You must not tell me what to do,' Jesus replied. 'My time has not yet come.'
>
> Jesus' mother then told the servants, 'Do whatever he tells you.'
>
> The Jews have rules about ritual washing, and for this purpose six stone water jars were there, each one large enough

to hold about a hundred litres. Jesus said to the servants, 'Fill these jars with water.' They filled them to the brim, and then he told them, 'Now draw some water out and take it to the man in charge of the feast.' They took him the water, which now had turned into wine, and he tasted it. He did not know where this wine had come from (but, of course, the servants who had drawn out the water knew); so he called the bridegroom and said to him, 'Everyone else serves the best wine first, and after the guests have had plenty to drink, he serves the ordinary wine. But you have kept the best wine until now!'

Jesus performed this first miracle in Cana in Galilee; he revealed his glory, and his disciples believed in him.

JOHN 2:1–11

Think or discuss

- The themes of glory and of faith (or believing) play an important part in John's Gospel. Jesus says, 'I have shown your glory on earth' (John 17:4), and John writes in his prologue, 'We saw his glory, the glory which he received as the Father's only Son' (John 1:14). The disciples saw Jesus' glory, or his power, in the 'sign' of water-into-wine and this led towards their faith and trust in him. Experiences of all sorts can lead to a vivid awareness of the reality and power of God. How can we use the signs and symbols around us, and the children's own experiences, to deepen their faith?
- Jesus' actions must have puzzled his disciples, but the miracle changed their view of him for ever. Do we feel bound to explain how or why God does everything or can we simply say, 'I don't know, but isn't it wonderful'?
- Jesus took something ordinary (water) and transformed it into wine, the sign of restoration and celebration. What place does worship and praise play in our children's work?
- Do the leaders or children in your church have talents or interests that could be used within worship?

Case study: Hot cross fun

You have always had a 'fun morning' on Good Friday, when the children make Easter cards and bunnies, and eat hot cross buns. Most of the children who come do not attend church frequently. This year, your new vicar wants the morning to start with a family service and for the children's activities to end by their taking part in a short procession of witness. Some of the parents have said that they think that the crucifixion is too nasty for children and they should only learn about Easter Day.

- How do you react to the suggested plans and the comments arising from them?
- What are the opportunities presented by the new plans?
- What difficulties might arise?
- How can you use the church building, and the signs and symbols connected with the Passion, in the session?

❖

Further action

Make a mental or written index of the ways that your church building can be used for teaching, and the various resources connected with the Christian year.

Do not use all your discoveries at once. Work out a strategy for using them to add a focus to your sessions, rather like adding spice or seasoning to food.

Consider using Lectionary-based teaching material if you do not already. Make the children aware of the colours, signs and symbols associated with the Christian year.

❖

Prayer

Let all the world in every corner sing,
My God and King!
The heavens are not too high,
His praise may thither fly;
The earth is not too low,
His praises there may grow.
Let all the world in every corner sing,
My God and King!

GEORGE HERBERT (1593–1632)

❖

Achievements

You should now be able to:

- Recognize and use the many teaching opportunities within the church building.
- Make positive use of the Christian year.
- Help the children to recognize God's glory through use of signs and symbols.

LITURGICAL COLOURS AND SYMBOLS

We all use colours to reflect our moods or to set an atmosphere, so it is hardly surprising that different colours have become associated with the events and seasons in the Church's year. Their use is increasing and going across all traditions. For centuries, a particular colour has been used on the lectern and pulpit, and the altar frontal, as well as the priest's stole and vestments. Banners and hangings have become popular recently, even in churches and chapels that do not normally use liturgical colours.

White and gold are colours of celebration, so they are used for the great feasts—Christmas, Easter, Trinity and All Saints' Day. They are also used for Candlemas and when remembering individual saints.

Red is the colour of fire, a sign of the Holy Spirit, so it is used at Pentecost. It is also the colour of blood, so is used for remembering saints who were martyred, and on Palm Sunday, Good Friday and Holy Cross day.

Purple is associated with penitence or sorrow, so it is used in Advent and Lent.

Green is used on every other occasion.

Common objects and symbols

1.	Advent	Advent wreath, Advent calendar
2.	Christmas	Crib, angels, star
3.	Epiphany	Star, gold, frankincense, myrrh
4.	Candlemas	Candles, Christingles
5.	Lent	Ashes, desert
6.	Holy Week	Palms, cross, objects associated with the crucifixion: nails, spear, robe, dice, crown of thorns
7.	Easter and Ascension	Cross, paschal candle, egg, empty tomb, garden
8.	Pentecost	Flames, wind, dove
9.	Harvest thanksgiving	Food, rain, sun, nature, industry.
10.	All Saints' tide	Lights, crowns, symbols associated with individual saints

WORSHIP AND SPIRITUALITY

UNIT A:
AN ENCOUNTER WITH THE LIVING GOD

Aims of the unit
- To explore ways of praying with children.
- To find ways of planning acts of worship.
- To discuss involving children in worship.

Bible passage: Mark 9:2–7

Introduction: What is worship?

Worship can be described as consciously putting oneself in the presence of God. It can be done anywhere and at any time, but the most effective way is when Christians meet together. It is important that your children have an experience of worshipping as part of the whole congregation, as well as having a time for worship that is appropriate for their age and culture.

The timing and style of your worship will depend on the context of your children's meeting. If it takes place as part of a Service of the Word or within a Eucharist, the children will be taking part in corporate worship already. You will want time for intercessions and some kind of penitential rite if you have not joined in one already. If the children are with you for the duration of the whole service, you will want opening and closing worship which includes praise, sorrow, thanksgiving and prayer for others.

Worship at a midweek or holiday club will need to be geared to the age and culture of the children, bearing in mind that many of them will have had no experience of prayer and little knowledge of God.

Setting the scene

Whatever the situation, your worship needs time and space. A quick prayer rattled together at an untidy table while the other leader clears up does nothing to build a child's relationship with God or encourage him in personal prayer. It teaches that worship is something to be fitted in at the last minute with little thought and less preparation—in short, it is not important. The setting of the room, posture of the children, and visual focus all help to make an atmosphere that is conducive to worship.

One of the major difficulties of worship within a Sunday or mid-week club is getting the children together. If the meeting starts in the hall, the children will not all arrive at the same time. There is similar tension at the end when one group is sitting ready while another is still clearing up. A rite of gathering can help to include everyone while setting a worshipful atmosphere. When some of the group have assembled, start to sing a simple repetitive song like 'Sing Hosanna'. As the children are hanging up coats, putting books away, they will join in. When the whole group has assembled, set the atmosphere by singing a last verse very quietly and then having a few seconds of silence.

Lord, teach us to pray

The word 'pray' originally meant 'to ask earnestly': 'I pray you, leave me alone.' It has developed from asking into being the word for reaching out to God. Our children need to see that it is natural to talk to God. The writer of the Genesis stories shows people having conversations, arguing, even making bargains with God—for example, when Abraham pleaded for Sodom to be spared from God's destruction (Genesis 18:16–32). Prayer is not confined to large books and antiquated language, neither is it a couple of especially written children's prayers, though that is part of it.

As we have seen in the previous unit, young children like repetition and pattern of worship. These can include special opening and closing prayers, a 'sorry' prayer, a hymn of praise, a special prayer for the group, and, of course, the Lord's Prayer. Hymns and songs that link with the Bible story or season of the year are also important.

Creative prayer

There are many ways of using the prayer time imaginatively. Sitting quietly in a dimmed room around a lighted candle and using music like Taizé chants is popular with older youngsters and adults alike. Some churches have a prayer board or box where people can post particular intercessions. Show it to the children and encourage them to use it, or make your own.

A powerful way of illustrating a penitential rite is to make a 'sin tree' by lightly fastening paper leaves, with sins written on them, to a branch. When a prayer for forgiveness is said, shake the branch lightly to illustrate God's removal of the burden of sin. Then decorate the tree with paper flowers to symbolize God's gift of new life. A similar rite uses rocks to represent sins, which are placed at the foot of the cross.

Children can write or draw their prayers and place them on the altar table. They can put Lenten resolutions in front of the cross or write 'love prayers' on hearts and lay them in front of the Christmas crib. Whatever the children offer, it is important to respect that these are their personal communications with God. Respect each child's privacy and do not comment on the prayer subjects or assess them in any way.

Thank you/Please

Every church service includes prayer for other people. That sometimes takes over from thanking God for his goodness to us. It can also mean that we are so busy telling God how to run the world that we forget to listen to him, to hear how he wants us to share in his saving work. An effective way of praying is for the children to say the things that have happened this week for which they want to thank God, and then the things that they want to tell him. These can be summed up with a silence for the children to make the prayers their own, finishing by saying the Lord's Prayer together.

❖

Think or discuss

- Brainstorm or note any other imaginative ways in which you have used prayer. Remember that the simplest ones are often the most effective.
- If you are working in a group, put everyone who works with the same age range or situation into pairs. Give each pair a season of the year: Advent, Easter, and so on.
- Ask each pair to design a short act of worship that lasts no longer than five or six minutes. Include the layout of your space, music, posture and prayers. Involve the children in leading it as appropriate.
- Share your plan with the rest of the meeting. Exchange comments and note down ideas. By the end of the meeting, you should have plans for several identified acts of worship.
- If you are using the material individually, lay out the framework for an act of worship and ask your fellow leaders to contribute their ideas.

We welcome you into the Lord's family

How do we really welcome children into our worship? Welcome is more than smiling at the children and knowing their names. It involves the attitude of the whole congregation. It means accepting that children do not behave the same way as adults and that they will want to join their parents, see what is going on and have the freedom to move about. They will want to join in the singing and prayers. In short, they will want to be as involved and happy as the adults are.

Unfortunately, many adults believe that children are not suitable people to be in church, especially at the Eucharist. It is not only possible, it is also essential to celebrate the Eucharist with children present, on at least some occasions. The Anglican tradition in particular has been to organize services as if only adults are going to be present and that attitude still holds strong in some people's minds. This is often hurtful for parents as well as their children. Children can be involved in worship in many ways that will help them to feel affirmed and be part of the Lord's family.

- Joining in the service as fully as possible.
- Showing and displaying work.
- Taking part in the offertory.
- Singing in the choir or being altar servers.
- Reading (see that the readings are appropriate and that children are given the opportunity to practise *in situ*).
- Leading the prayers (short bidding prayers on cards are best).
- Assisting the sidespeople by giving out service sheets and books.

There are many ways in which we can help children and their families:

- Greeting the children and seeing that they are offered books.
- Having at least one hymn that is familiar to children or easy to sing.
- Informing visitors about the various facilities.
- Having a crèche area in the church for toddlers.
- Providing children's service books and activity bags.
- Sitting with a parent who has young children.
- Listening to the children and accepting that we can learn from them too.
- Having a monthly service which is geared towards children and fringe members.

Think about or discuss the following questions:

- Which of the things listed do we do in our church?
- Which two others could we start to do?
- Do we really believe that children have things to give as well as receive?
- A church that takes its children seriously will always have a sense of vitality and hope through them. Is this your experience?
- However effective our welcome, parents will often feel self-conscious about the behaviour of their own children. How can we help them to feel relaxed?

Bible reading

Jesus took with him Peter, James, and John, and led them up a high mountain, where they were alone. As they looked on, a change came over Jesus, and his clothes became shining white —whiter than anyone in the world could wash them. Then the three disciples saw Elijah and Moses talking with Jesus. Peter spoke up and said to Jesus, 'Teacher, how good it is that we are here! We will make three tents, one for you, one for Moses, and one for Elijah.' He and the others were so frightened that he did not know what to say.

Then a cloud appeared and covered them with its shadow, and a voice came from the cloud, 'This is my own dear Son— listen to him!'

MARK 9:2–7

Think or discuss

- What glimpses of God do we see through the beauty of his world and people that we meet?
- How do we prepare our worship so that the children can experience the presence of God?
- 'This is my own dear Son—listen to him!' Do we allow time to listen to God?
- Are we equipping our children so that, when God calls them at some time in their lives, they will recognize his call and be able to respond to it?

❖

Case study: Angela's class assemblies

Angela taught in a church primary school in an inner city. Twice a week, she led her class's assembly. Rather than having the usual prayers, she simply said, 'What do you want to thank God for, children?' After collecting some of the good news of the week, she then asked the children what things they wanted to tell God. Out came the personal sadness and worries and some items from the television news. Quietly, Angela continued, 'Let's put all those things into God's hands.' After a few seconds of silence, they all said the Lord's Prayer together. As the months passed, the class became highly aware of local and international issues and needs. They sent cards to the wife of an imprisoned hostage. They reported improvements in the Ethiopian famine. They even asked to stop to say a prayer outside the Funeral Directors on the way to swimming.

- Why do you think this style of prayer was effective?
- Do you think that it affected the children's personal prayer?
- How could you use this with your children's work?
- How would you handle any difficult or sensitive issues that may arise from this style of prayer?

Further action

Review the way that you plan and lead your worship with children.

Try encouraging the children to mention any matters that concern them during the prayers. If this is not appropriate, have two ice-cream boxes, one for thanksgivings, the other for petitions. Invite the children to put in any subjects for prayers. Use them in the closing worship. This can be done without revealing individually sensitive requests.

Look critically at your Sunday service. Are there any ways that it could be more appropriate for children without marginalizing the adults?

Prayer
God, our Father,
you showed Jesus in his transfigured glory to his friends
and commanded them to listen to him.
Teach us how to listen to you and to each other,
so that we shall come to understand your plan for us,
and show your glory in our lives.

We make our prayer through your Son, Jesus Christ,
who lives and reigns in glory with you and the Holy Spirit,
one God for ever and ever.

Achievements

You should now be able to:

- Plan a simple act of worship.
- Use imaginative ways of praying with children.
- Find appropriate ways of involving the children in the Sunday worship.

UNIT B:
GROWING FAITH

Aims of the unit
- To gain a basic knowledge of the way that children develop spiritually.
- To discuss the issues and challenges of helping children to grow in faith.
- To touch upon the importance of leaders' own spiritual development.

Bible passage: Luke 2:41–52

Introduction: Growing faith

The final verse of this unit's Bible reading describes the boy Jesus as growing, 'both in body and in wisdom, gaining favour with God and people'. It sums up the way that children develop as whole people, physically, mentally and also spiritually and socially. We need to take all these aspects of child development into our children's nurture. There is not the space for a detailed discussion of spiritual development in this book, but many other resources deal with this subject in more detail.

There are stages in spiritual development as much as in physical, mental and social development. The tendency is to welcome and encourage physical, mental and social growth, a child's first steps, learning to read and making friends. As children grow older, we celebrate their growing tall, passing exams, going on holiday with friends, and it is natural to hope that they will eventually travel, leave home and have their own families. We worry if they are slow to talk, do not relate well to other children or show no interest in the world around them.

Unfortunately, we do not take the same care with our children's spiritual development. We tend to assume that it will develop automatically as the children grow up or, worse still, we positively discourage the 'growing pains' that accompany the testing of a faith. James

Fowler's research into faith development in the 1970s identified six stages of faith. He noted that many adults did not develop beyond the third stage, the 'conforming faith' of many teenagers. Another American researcher, John Westerhoff, distinguished the following four styles of faith:

Experienced faith

'I feel.' The young child senses love and acceptance that gives a setting for faith to form. Patterns and routines strengthen this framework and give a sense of security.

Affiliative faith

'I belong.' Worshipping in a community gives a sense of belonging. Adult members of the faith community are seen as 'good'. The child notes and copies their teaching and behaviour. Experience of awe and wonder, learning faith stories from scripture, all help to deepen faith. There is a strong need to belong and to identify with fellow believers.

Searching faith

'Who am I?' This is a time of questioning and searching about oneself as much as about one's faith. It can be linked to the adolescent years. Previously accepted values can come under scrutiny. Critical judgment and honest doubt are a vital part of this process that can lead to the development of a personal faith.

Owned faith or mature faith

'Here I stand.' The sense of belonging, combined with the results of the period of searching, allows the person to stand up for what they believe and to put their faith into action. They are secure enough to be open to other people's points of view. They continue to explore and enrich their own faith.

Unlike physical and mental development, however, we constantly revisit these four stages of faith. A serious personal crisis, major illness or bereavement can take a person right back to the stage of needing love and acceptance, with the familiar forms and patterns of worship to sustain them while they recover. 'I could not take anything in; I just clung to the words' is a common statement from people in this situation.

Many people's faith remains at the affiliative stage. These people will be committed and loyal, maybe working tirelessly for the parish. On the other hand, they may find new theological perspectives disturbing and be resistant to changes in the church building or service. In an extreme form, the person may stop attending church if they move house and find that the local church has a different tradition from the one that they have always attended.

Some young people may demonstrate a relationship with God that is apparently more mature than that of many adults. That does not mean, however, that they will not need the familiar patterns of worship and constant reassurance that they are valued members of the Christian community. They will also go through the periods of questioning and doubt.

Some youngsters will find the time of doubt very difficult if their faith has not been encouraged to grow through the affiliative stage. Past teaching is perceived to be flawed and childish, so, in some cases, the whole Christian story is dismissed with other childish things.

A person with mature faith will still have times of questioning, and will always need the support of a Christian community where he or she is respected and valued.

The pattern of faith development is, therefore, rather like a spiral. The person revisits the various stages but looks at them from a slightly different angle as he or she gets older and gains different experiences of life.

Think or discuss

- *'I feel.'* Does your children's group have an atmosphere of love and acceptance? How can this be mirrored in the larger church community?
- *'I belong.'* Are there opportunities for the children or adults on the fringe to gain a sense of belonging? This can be through participating in a variety of ways, including worship and social events.

- *'Who am I?'* How does your church encourage people to have a sense of self-worth, to express their doubts and ask questions?
- *'Here I stand.'* Westerhoff describes this as mature faith. How can people be encouraged to continue on their spiritual journeys and eventually own their faith?

You will find several books on this subject listed at the end of this book, should you want to research further (see Appendix B).

Basic spiritual development: a guide

The following notes give a basic guide to helping children to develop spiritually.

Up to about seven years

Children aged up to about seven years have a powerful sense of the presence and wonder of God. They have a vivid imagination and take stories and symbols literally, confusing fact and fiction. Ghosts, fairies and, indeed, God are as real as things that are tangible.

As they develop mentally, they start to ask questions about the nature of God. Some of these are based on the supposition that God is like a person; others can be deep theological questions: 'What does God eat for breakfast?' 'What would have happened if Jesus had not been crucified?'

They experience love and care from their parents and they start to form relationships.

They enjoy the pattern and repetition of worship and join in the prayers and music by copying the adults around them.

Eight plus

This is the age when children's spontaneous belief in God changes, coinciding with their going through a latent emotional period. They become less clinging and affectionate to their mothers or carers. They are no longer anxious to please their parents and teachers. They start to get their own ideas and make their own decisions. 'Let me help' becomes 'Why should I?' or 'Can we do something different?' They also start to sort out fact from fiction, to ask, 'Is it true?' Stories and symbols are still taken literally. Leaders need to be careful when teaching some Old Testament stories and dealing with abstract concepts like heaven and hell.

Children of this age will have started to realize that, as Christians, they are in a minority among their school friends. They will need support and care from their families and the Christian community if they are to resist peer pressure and remain part of the Church.

Trying and testing
Older children will start to test their faith (and yours) with questions about the authenticity of scripture, the power of prayer and the problems of pain, hunger and war. These are signs that the youngsters are growing up, and we should welcome them rather than seeing them as difficulties.

Be ready for a searching or provocative question by having thought through the possible questions yourself as part of preparing a session. Ensure that your answer is appropriate for the level of the child's understanding. Do not be afraid to say that you do not know the answer, but that you will try to find out. Teach the context of a Bible passage to the older children. Challenge them with your questions and accept their challenges to you, uncomfortable though they may be.

Much of scripture is an explanation of the inexplicable. We tell stories as a way of probing great truths. The rabbinical tradition of teaching, of which Jesus was a part, is to explain a truth with a story, like a parable, and then explain that story with another one; to answer a question with another question. That way, the listener is always searching and wondering.

What is truth?
We also need to differentiate between scientific, historical and spiritual truth. Whether an event really happened or whether there is scientific information to support it or not are only partial measures of truth. The principal aim of studying scripture is to find out the truth that it teaches about the nature of God and his relationship with us. We will discuss preparing to teach a Bible story and the techniques of storytelling in Unit 4A.

Letting go

Bringing up a child is a process of letting go. At first the child has to be carried, then he learns to crawl independently. The next stage is walking, followed several years later by going on short walks from home. Travelling by public transport follows, often with the youngster planning his own route. In the late teens, many youngsters learn to drive, and may disappear for months to travel the world. Whether or not the young person achieves all of this without mishap depends largely on the appropriateness of the training and guidance that the parents gave him. There is a balance between allowing a toddler to play by a main road and taking him everywhere by car when he is sixteen.

It is the same with faith development. Unfortunately, we do not always recognize this. Faith has to be helped to grow and eventually to be owned. Whether it flourishes into a mature faith, withers from lack of sustenance or takes a twist into an extreme cult depends much on the appropriateness of the teaching and guidance that the child has received. Questions and doubts are part of growing up and finding one's own identity. Some youngsters may make some kind of Christian commitment, like confirmation; others will disappear and may return years later. Our task as leaders is to nurture the seeds of faith and accept that we may not see them come to fruition.

Membership

Just as children soon have a sense of being part of a family, they should feel that they are an equal and valued part of the Christian community. This is undermined if the Junior Church is badly equipped or the nurture is poor. It is belied if the children are greeted with frowns and 'Sh!' when they creep into the service or if the social events are for adults only. Knowing and using children's names, taking an interest in their achievements, involving them in worship and other events, are vital if the children are to keep their sense of being part of God's family. When the testing time comes, youngsters need to know that they are still loved and accepted, that leaders have time for them and that adults of all ages also ask questions and have doubts.

- Do we rejoice as our children's faith develops, or do we want to freeze it at the 'sweet and simple' stage?
- Do we see the questions and restlessness from our older children as a desire to grow spiritually or a problem that we cannot tackle?
- Is our teaching appropriate for the age and experience of the children that we lead?
- Is our own faith constantly being tested and renewed?
- 'When I was a child, my speech, feelings, and thinking were all those of a child; now that I have grown up, I have no more use for childish ways. What we see now is like a dim image in a mirror; then we shall see face to face. What I know now is only partial; then it will be complete—as complete as God's knowledge of me' (1 Corinthians 13:11–12). God does not change, but our understanding of him has changed through history and will continue to change throughout our lives. We will not know him fully in this life. How does this affect the nurture of our children?

Our own faith

There is an old saying that the faith is caught, not taught. So far, we have concentrated on teaching about the faith. The best teacher, however, is the example of the whole congregation and the children's leaders in particular. Think back to your own coming to faith. You will probably find that the strongest influences were people themselves, rather than anything that they taught you.

- Is the God you know and worship the same God as the one you teach?
- Do you set a good example to the children by the way you behave?
- Can you admit your own spiritual doubts, failures and difficulties?
- Do you top up your own spiritual batteries with regular worship and personal prayer?
- Do you help your own faith to develop by joining a study group, using Bible reading notes, having a spiritual director or going on an occasional quiet day?

If the answer to any of these is 'No', do not just push it aside as unnecessary or think that you are an unsuitable children's leader. You will probably find help in addressing the first three questions by using the support contained in the fourth and fifth questions.

Bible reading

Read this account of a young man starting to act independently and testing his faith.

Every year the parents of Jesus went to Jerusalem for the Passover Festival. When Jesus was twelve years old, they went to the festival as usual. When the festival was over, they started back home, but the boy Jesus stayed in Jerusalem. His parents did not know this; they thought that he was with the group, so they travelled a whole day and then started looking for him among their relatives and friends. They did not find him, so they went back to Jerusalem looking for him. On the third day they found him in the Temple, sitting with the Jewish teachers, listening to them and asking questions. All who heard him were amazed at his intelligent answers. His parents were astonished when they saw him, and his mother said to him, 'My son, why have you done this to us? Your father and I have been terribly worried trying to find you.'

He answered them, 'Why did you have to look for me? Didn't you know that I had to be in my Father's house?' But they did not understand his answer.

So Jesus went back with them to Nazareth, where he was obedient to them. His mother treasured all these things in her heart. Jesus grew both in body and in wisdom, gaining favour with God and people.

LUKE 2:41–52

Think or discuss

- Jesus was found in the Temple, 'sitting with the Jewish teachers, listening to them and asking questions'. Do we allow time for questions? How do we react if a child asks a question that challenges us or shows that he/she is questioning or exploring his/her faith?

- 'All who heard him were amazed at his intelligent answers.' Do we listen to children and include their answers and remarks into our teaching? Do we take our children seriously as ministers of Christ? Do we believe in our heart of hearts that God does speak to us through children?
- 'Didn't you know that I had to be in my Father's house?' This is Luke's record of Jesus' first words. In previous passages, Mary, Gabriel, angels and Simeon have said who he is. Now Jesus says it himself. He is already conforming to God's will. What implications does this have on our own ministries?
- 'Jesus grew both in body and in wisdom, gaining favour with God and people.' Do we see our children as whole people, or are they empty buckets to be filled with knowledge? Do we encourage them to develop, or do we try to defer it in order to avoid challenges and problems?

Case study: Young Martins spread their wings

St Martin's church had very few children until five years ago. Now it has regular contact with about 25 youngsters. The oldest ones have just started secondary school. The leader has detected a certain disaffection among them. Some of this is inconsistent. It includes complaining about having to go into church because the adults stare at them, but saying in the next breath that Sunday school is only for babies. Last week the children were preparing for the Harvest Thanksgiving by reading Genesis chapter 1, the creation story. One reaction was, 'How can any sensible person still believe that the world was created in a week?'

- Using the information you have gained from this unit and your own experience, discuss ways in which you can support these youngsters.
- What suggestions do you have for dealing with their complaints concerning the format on Sunday?

- How can you affirm their sense of being a valued part of the Christian community?
- Brainstorm ways of responding to their reaction to the Genesis story. How can you give the youngsters time and space to deal with these issues?

Further action

- Make notes of the main phases of children's spiritual development. Check that they are consistent with the way you teach specific age groups.
- Think about ways in which you can meet the spiritual needs of each member of your group. Remember that their age and intellect may not necessarily reflect their stage of spiritual growth.
- Think about the way you answer the tricky question. Be prepared to give time and thought. Note that the best response to many questions is to ask another question, thus prompting discussion.
- Look at your own spiritual life. Resolve to act upon one part of it. This may involve asking for advice.

Prayer

Lord, you have examined me and you know me...
You created every part of me;
you put me together in my mother's womb.
I praise you because you are to be feared;
all you do is strange and wonderful.
I know it with all my heart.
When my bones were being formed,
carefully put together in my mother's womb,
when I was growing there in secret,
you knew that I was there—
you saw me before I was born.
The days allocated to me
had all been recorded in your book,

before any of them ever began.
O Lord, how precious are your thoughts to me,
how many of them there are!
If I counted them, they would be
more than the grains of sand.
When I awake, I am still with you.

PSALM 139:1, 13–18

Achievements

You should now be able to:
- Discern something of the ways that children develop spiritually.
- Address some of the issues and challenges of helping children to grow in faith.
- Understand the importance of listening to and answering questions about spiritual matters.

THE PLACE OF STORY

Unit A:
The word of the Lord

Aims of the unit
- To look at imaginative ways of using the Bible.
- To discover various storytelling techniques.
- To address the challenge of explaining the unexplainable.

Bible passage: Mark 4:30–33

Introduction: God's storybook

The Bible is a collection of books in one binding. The first part, the Old Testament, is the story of God's relationship with the Jewish people: their laws and history, their great leaders and prophets, good people and villains. It also contains legends and proverbs, poetry and songs. Some of the stories cover centuries; others are just a few sentences long. It all adds up to one great story: how God gradually revealed himself to his people, his covenant (or 'testament') with them, and how they responded through the centuries.

The New Testament is the story of how God revealed himself through the life, death and resurrection of Jesus Christ. It shows how some people recognized him as God's Son and began to follow him. This is recorded in the four Gospels—Matthew, Mark, Luke and John. They form the historical basis of our faith. The continuing story of his followers, his Church, is told in the book of Acts, and letters, or 'epistles', in which great Christian leaders sent news, teaching and guidance to groups of early Christians. But the story is not finished. It has continued through two thousand years and we are part of it.

If our children are to grow in the fellowship of God's people, the Church, they need to hear and receive the story in a way that is accessible and relevant. This will only happen if you know and value it and have some understanding of the passages you are teaching. If it has little meaning to you beyond being an account that was written thousands of years ago about some people of a different age and culture from ours, it will not interest or excite your children.

Before planning a session, read the Bible passage a couple of times. Then look at it from your own experience. For example, take a short Bible passage like Luke 6:43-45.

'A healthy tree does not bear bad fruit, nor does a poor tree bear good fruit. Every tree is known by the fruit it bears; you do not pick figs from thorn bushes or gather grapes from bramble bushes. A good person brings good out of the treasure of good things from his heart; a bad person brings bad out of the treasure of bad things. For the mouth speaks what the heart is full of.'

Think or discuss

If you are working individually, assemble your thoughts in your mind and, in a silent space, ask God to speak to you through them. If you are working with a group, share your images after a short period of silence.

Read the passage through a couple of times. What thoughts and feelings are called to mind? Look at the verses surrounding the passage so that you understand the context in which it is placed. Close your eyes and imagine that you are there.

- What does this scene look like?
- What has somebody said or done to make Jesus tell this tale?
- What trees or plants are there for him to use as visual aids?
- How are his listeners reacting?
- How does this passage link with things that have happened to you, or with your beliefs or your lifestyle?
- What does the passage say to you about God and his people? Are there things that you had not noticed before?

When you have thought about these things or discussed them, start to plan how you will present the story to the children. Their experience is also part of the whole story. The smallest children will know that various fruits 'belong' to their trees; older ones may have noticed things about the quality of fruit by helping with gardening or just being observant. At a deeper level, they will all have had experience of people saying cruel or kind things, making suggestions that lead to good results or others that cause trouble and misery. Use the following questions to help you to make your plan.

- What experiences in your children's lives can you call to mind that will help with the teaching of this passage?
- Is there anything in your surroundings that you can use as an illustration, like a horse chestnut or sycamore tree outside the church?
- Think about communication. What do you want the children to learn? How will you get this across?
- Think about the shape of the session. What would be the best point to introduce the passage? What would be a good introductory activity? How will you finish?
- After the session, will you have taught another Bible story or will you have helped the children to understand a story they may already know and to apply it to their lives?
- Most important, will the teaching have helped the children to grow in their faith and understanding of God?

Being a Christian involves having a relationship with Jesus and following his teaching and example. The Bible, especially the Gospels, is our record and guide. Even the youngest child can understand the significance of Jesus taking children in his arms, healing the sick, enjoying meals with his friends, and throwing the extortioners out of the temple. If the Bible is important to us, we will communicate that to our children. Our enthusiasm and awareness of God's loving presence in our lives should fire them. This is more important than lengthy explanations.

Telling stories

We all enjoy a good story. Storytelling has been used in every age and culture to teach profound truths by relating them to everyday events, or using fantasy and imagery to try to explain the inexplicable. Jesus based much of his teaching on stories about people, places and situations he knew. His listeners immediately knew and recognized people like a landowner with a tearaway son; farmers watching their corn grow; two builders, one with a plot of hard rock, the other trying to build a safe dwelling on sand. Story grows out of life, so children who read and listen can find their experiences confirmed, challenged, developed and broadened.

All of our teaching must be rooted in scripture, but using stories of people who lived in the Middle East several thousands of years ago can detach them from everyday life in the mind of a child. They are different, difficult or even dull. However, Jesus' stories are timeless, and many of the tales of the Old Testament teach us things about God's relationship with his people that can be paralleled with our lives today. They also provide the backdrop to the Gospels.

So, how do we tell our Bible stories?

- Do we use appropriate versions of scripture for the children's levels of understanding?
- Is the Bible we use accessible and visually attractive?
- How do we tell a Bible story? Have we rehearsed it so that the children are interested and excited by it? Do not fall into the trap of explaining the point of the story before you start, or labouring it at the end. The message should emerge in the telling of the tale and the days ahead when the child recalls it.
- Do we ever fall into the trap of distancing the story from reality: 'Long, long ago, in a far-off land, there lived a man with a funny name that I can't pronounce...'?
- Have we looked at words or situations that may need adapting or unpacking during the story? How do we set about this?
- Do we ever tell the story in our own words? Sitting and talking to the children with the Bible on our laps or placed beside us gives a very powerful message.

- The Bible is very important. Some churches place it open on the table as the focal point of worship; others carry it in procession with candles. How do we demonstrate its importance to the children?
- If you are in a group, brainstorm on lively ways to communicate the faith through story.

Storytelling techniques

The way that we read can have a profound effect on the listener for good or ill. Perhaps the Bible suffers more than any other book from poor and unimaginative reading. Everyone can develop storytelling skills:

- Sit on a level with the children. Engage them with your eyes.
- If you are with a large group, look alternately at the two back corners. That way, you keep eye contact with everyone.
- A story is a dialogue with your audience. Even if they do not speak, the children will respond with their eyes, facial expressions, and body language.
- Get your head out of the book. Take in a sentence and then look at your listeners as you speak.
- Most people read too fast. Slow down, not by speaking more slowly but by pausing at commas and full stops.
- Show your emotions in your voice, facial expression, body language and gestures.
- Engage with the story by trying to imagine it as you tell it.
- The most important part of a story is the first sentence. See that it attracts the children's attention. If you are reading from scripture, you may have to adapt the opening phrase. 'After that, he said...' is not an effective start to a story. Make a habit of memorizing or writing out your opening sentence.
- See that the story has a clear and neat ending.

Bible reading

'What shall we say the Kingdom of God is like?' asked Jesus. 'What parable shall we use to explain it? It is like this. A man takes a mustard seed, the smallest seed in the world, and plants it in the ground. After a while it grows up and becomes the biggest of all plants. It puts out such large branches that the birds come and make their nests in its shade.'

Jesus preached his message to the people, using many other parables like these; he told them as much as they could understand.

MARK 4:30–33

Think or discuss

- A mustard seed is very tiny but produces an umbrella-shaped shrub that stands about three metres tall. Farming, however, is not a simple process. It takes patience and consistent care. It also includes disappointment and failure. Are we impatient for spectacular or quick results in our work with children?
- Jesus used a handy visual aid to teach a great truth. Imagine him picking up a seed from the dust, placing it on his finger, then pointing to the tree. Do we have that immediacy in our teaching?
- How can we best present Jesus' teaching to our children, given their different ages and levels of understanding?
- What methods do we use to discern how much our children can understand?

Case study: Friday night panic!

Judith has been helping with a group of 7–8 year olds for several Sundays. Next week she is leading the group because the usual leader is on holiday. She telephones you, very worried because the leader has forgotten to leave the teaching book with her. She knows that the Gospel reading is Mark 4:30–33, Jesus' description of the kingdom of God being like a mustard seed. She would like advice on ways of teaching the 30-minute session.

- Using the information you have gained from this unit, advise Judith on an effective way of telling the story.
- What is the English equivalent of a small seed growing into a large tree? Can you use it in this session?
- Add visual aids, drama and music if appropriate.
- Design a simple activity to reinforce the story.
- Give Judith a clear opening to the story and a way of summing up and closing the session.

Further action

- Improve your storytelling skills by telling stories in different ways to your group. If you have the opportunity to watch yourself on video or even tell stories to a mirror, this can be very helpful.
- Find what OHP, tape recorder or video equipment is available and see that you can use it effectively.

The advice given in this chapter is just a beginning. There are two ways forward—first to practise and second to watch professional storytellers on television or video. Note their facial expressions, body language and, most of all, their timing.

Prayer

Almighty God,
We thank you for the gift of your holy word.
May it be a lantern to our feet,
a light to our paths,
and a strength to our lives.
Take us and use us
to love and serve
in the power of your Holy Spirit
and in the name of your Son, Jesus Christ our Lord.
PATTERNS FOR WORSHIP

❖

Achievements

You should now be able to:

- Study a Bible passage as part of your preparation for a session.
- Use the Bible in an attractive way that allows the children to experience the presence and love of God through reading his word.
- Apply with effect some simple storytelling techniques.

UNIT B:
MIME, MUSIC AND MOVEMENT

Aims of the unit
- To look at some of the various skills that can be a means of enhancing our storytelling.
- To explore further the concept of learning with the whole person.
- To think about using the talents of people who are not directly involved in children's work.

Bible passage: Psalm 136:1–9, 26

Introduction: Media to help with storytelling

This unit is rather different from previous ones. It contains information on ways of using various arts as media in our telling of God's story, but, because the topics are essentially practical, it is incomplete. It reviews some of the ways in which we can use various arts in our work. It also introduces some activities that are deliberately designed to encourage the nervous and provide a light relief from the more serious discussion of the other units. There is no case study. Each activity becomes a case study in itself as the group discusses it or the individual thinks about ways of using it.

You may decide that you want to study one particular skill as a group, either because it is something you are all eager to improve upon or because you have an expert who can teach you. You could also choose your own subject and work on that alone or with a partner. Whatever you choose, use the opportunity for anyone in the group with particular skills and talents to teach something to his or her companions. You can also use this opportunity to identify and draw in people from your community who have particular skills that they can pass on to you or directly to the children by helping with the children's work on occasions. There are several books and details of organizations to give you more information on each subject at the end of the book (see Appendices B and C).

If you are working alone, you may feel tempted to skip this unit. Try to read it through in a spirit of enquiry. It may urge you to start to use a skill that you have set aside or to take up an interest that has been in your mind for some time.

You will probably not work on everything in this unit. If you are working in a group, read each section through before the meeting and ask yourself these three questions:

* Am I good enough at any of these skills to use them in my children's work?
* Which skill do I think that I could start to use if I had some training?
* Who in our church has a particular skill that he or she could use in our children's work occasionally? Could this include providing some training for us?

Take your answers back to your group or fellow leaders.

Drama

Bible stories have been dramatized for centuries as a way of teaching them to people who could not read. Many churches still read or sing the Passion story dramatically on Palm Sunday and Good Friday. Nativity plays are even more popular. Children and young people will gain a great deal from drama, and can use it in a service or at a social event. Consider the following suggestions.

* Use one of the many books of biblical plays that are suitable for children.
* Act out a Bible passage by someone reading the story while the actors mime it. Timing is crucial, so, unless the reader can see the actors clearly, you will need someone to indicate when he or she should pause in the narrative, and when to move on.
* Read the story in parts. This involves little preparation if the youngsters are fluent readers. Mark the parts with a highlighter pen or invest in a copy of the *Dramatised Bible*.

- Create your own modern parable by retelling and acting the story as if Jesus were telling it today. Working it out can be a powerful way of unpacking the truths behind the story.
- Tell the story in your own words as if it had just happened and you had been an observer. Think how you would have seen the action if you had been Pilate's servant watching your master try to uphold law and order while convinced that Jesus was not guilty. Think how you would have felt if you were Jairus' wife, left alone to nurse your dying daughter while Jairus goes for help. It gives a completely new dimension to the story.

Activity

If you are working in a group, work in twos or threes. It will work equally well if you are using this material individually. You could enlist the help of a fellow leader or member of your family to use as your audience.

Take one of the following Bible passages or one of the two examples in the previous paragraph. Imagine you were there and the event had just happened. Tell the story in your own way. This could be just one person speaking or an interview, or you could act it out. Say how you feel and how people around you behaved. Remember about starting with a clear sentence to get your audience interested and then rounding the story off neatly.

- You are a rabbi in the temple in Jerusalem. A young lad keeps turning up and asking questions. Then his parents appear... (Luke 2:46–50).
- You are a young man who likes living life to the full. Your best friend is getting married, but then the drink starts to run out... (John 2:1–11).
- You are a child in a crowd, listening to Jesus. It is getting late. Everyone is hungry, and the leaders are asking people to give their food for sharing out. You call out, 'Please, you can have my lunch...' (Mark 6:30–44).
- You are Mary, who has experienced the agony of seeing her son tortured and crucified. Some of his friends are convinced that somehow he is still with them...

Music

Many people think that music is too difficult for anyone besides a specialist to lead or to teach. Children's work leaders happily produce the most imaginative craft work and enthral youngsters with stories or drama but become reduced to nervous wrecks at the very suggestion that they should lead a simple song. There are all sorts of reasons for this reticence, which usually come down to a lack of confidence and experience.

Songs stay in people's minds because the melody and rhythm help the performers to retain them. Singing is also a good way of helping the children to feel that they belong together. Much of the reticence about teaching singing springs from lack of confidence. If you follow some basic techniques, the children should respond and your confidence will grow. Believe in the voice that God has given you and be prepared to have a go.

- Sit on the same level as the children. Make sure that you can see and be seen by everyone. Look at the children while you sing to them and smile.
- Only teach songs that you have sung through until you know them well. Find out what hymn/song books most of the children use at school and start by using some of their favourites.
- Sing a line at a time using your flattened hand to show the pitch of the notes. People generally find it easier to imitate another voice than a guitar, piano or organ.
- Explain the structure of the song: for example, 'The second line is like the first but it goes down at the end.' This allows the children to learn with their minds as well as their eyes and ears.
- Teach action songs by saying the words in the rhythm while doing the actions. The actions fit with the rhythm of the words and aid memory. Add the tune last of all.
- If you feel that you must have an instrument, just play the melody line. Only add an accompaniment when the children know the melody.
- Believe that your youngsters can respond well... and they will. If something does not go well, make it into a joke and challenge the children to do better... and they will.

A piano is not a good instrument for accompanying children unless you have a capable pianist. A guitar or keyboard is better because you can play without losing eye contact with the singers.

Taped music is useful for setting an atmosphere or learning a tune but singing with it is difficult because of leaving time to breathe and ensuring a good attack at the beginning of verses. Many children are capable musicians and enjoy using their skills. A teenage helper may be well capable of leading music on a melodic instrument if you give him or her time to practise or take the music to a lesson. Ask your organist to help by giving you a list of the music being sung in church and making you a tape of any new hymns or songs if you have no one to play them for you.

Activity
Get a member of the group, or somebody in your worship team, to teach you all a simple song using the above methods. Once you have the idea, let several people have a go. If you can teach singing to your friends, you should find it easy with a group of youngsters.

Poetry

People remember poetry as easily as music because of its rhythm, rhyming and regular metre. So, teach poetry! The Bible is full of poems. The book of Psalms, the songs of Zechariah and Mary in Luke 1, and the creation story in Genesis 1 are some of the most well-known poetic passages. Read them to the children with the pace and metre of poetry. If there is a regular response, like 'Evening passed and morning came—that was the first day' (Genesis 1:5), encourage the children to join in.

Use hymns or songs based on Bible passages to consolidate the story. Read them if you cannot manage to sing them. The hymn writer Mrs C.F. Alexander wrote her hymns as a way of teaching children about the faith in a way that they could understand and retain. Some of them are very dated but those like 'There is a green hill' and 'Once in royal David's city' have become part of our culture. There are several books of poems on biblical subjects for young children. These include actions and simple finger games. You can even try making up your own verses. The easiest way is to base your poem on a well-known hymn. That will give you a strong and regular metre as well as a linguistic framework.

Activity
Divide the group into pairs or threes. Ask each group to make up a limerick based on a biblical character. If you are using the material individually, you might like to try out your efforts on family members, friends or fellow leaders. For example:

> *A rabbi from Tarsus named Saul*
> *Didn't like early Christians at all,*
> *Till he saw the Lord's light,*
> *It gave him a fright,*
> *Then he wrote lots of letters signed, 'Paul'.*

Puppets

Puppets have been used in Christian teaching for several centuries. The traditional Punch and Judy show had Christian origins. In the Middle Ages, street parades and plays included larger than life-sized puppets representing biblical characters. These were made of cross-pieces of wood with a head attached to the top and cloth wrapped around for clothes. They were very effective and popular.

If you can learn to handle a puppet, this can be an enormous assistance in storytelling. Give it a name and a character so that the children can relate to it. You can tell the story by using it for questions and answers. It can interrupt, make comments, and even be cheeky. 'Henry is talking behind his hand. That is rude. I know. Shall I tell him to stop?' It can also be your mask. If you feel self-conscious, you can hide behind the puppet's character or have a conversation with it.

Professionally made puppets are beautiful but expensive. If you use them regularly and allow them to develop a character, they are a good investment. But before investing in one, try making your own. This is not as difficult as you may think.

Make glove puppets from socks or mittens with faces embroidered on them or with felt features stuck on with glue.

Stick puppets are even easier. Draw a face on a wooden spoon and stick on some wool for hair, or use a paper plate taped to a stick.

The simplest method of all is to draw a face on the centre of a kitchen roll, or a paper bag.

The important thing is to give the puppet a name and a character so that the children can relate to it.

Activity

Make a simple puppet and practise talking with it. As with singing, try your new techniques on the others in your group or your family before using them on the children. You will probably feel very self-conscious at first, but try to forget about your feelings. Even be prepared to have a good laugh at your own efforts!

Visual aids

Visual symbols have been used in worship to help to teach about the nature of God for centuries. Robes, candles and processions all add to the sense of occasion, the sense that worship is something special. Signs such as vividly coloured vestments create a rich environment for taking in the meaning and mystery of worship.

As we discussed in Unit 2B, the church building in itself is a wonderful visual aid. Familiarize yourself with your church so that you can use the various aids naturally. Even if you are meeting in the church hall, tell the children that there is a stained-glass window or other furnishing that is linked with the story and show it to them when they go into church.

Good-quality pictures, maps and OHP acetates may also add interest to a story. Many of the Gospel stories revolve around visual aids—seeds, bread and fish, a lost coin. Find the objects that are the pivot of the story and display them. Pass them around so that the children can handle, smell or taste them.

Thanks to photocopiers and computers, it is relatively easy to provide high-quality pictures. See that they are clear and easily visible to the whole group. If they are very large, mount them on cardboard.

Activity

Divide the group into pairs. Give each pair the title of something that is frequently seen in church. Ask them to make up a couple of sentences explaining it in language that a child of about eight would understand. Then, second, suggest a Bible story or piece of teaching where this might be a useful visual aid.

Subjects could include the cross, font, altar or table, water, candle, stained-glass window of Jesus carrying a lamb, hassock with embroidered crossed keys.

❖

Bible reading

Rather than studying this passage in the usual way, just find an interesting way of reading it and think about ways in which you could use art, music or dramatic reading to enhance the poetry.

Give thanks to the Lord, because he is good;
his love is eternal.
Give thanks to the greatest of all gods;
his love is eternal.
Give thanks to the mightiest of all lords;
his love is eternal.

He alone performs great miracles;
his love is eternal.
By his wisdom he made the heavens;
his love is eternal;
he built the earth on the deep waters;
his love is eternal.
He made the sun and the moon;
his love is eternal;
the sun to rule over the day;
his love is eternal;
the moon and the stars to rule over the night;
his love is eternal...

Give thanks to the God of heaven;
his love is eternal.

PSALM 136:1–9, 26

Further action

- Choose one skill that you think you could use more in your work.
- Choose a second skill that you could start to use a little with guidance.
- If one of your congregation has a particular skill, ask if he or she would be willing to provide your group with some training one evening. Your diocese or region may also provide training courses.

Prayer

Father, you spoke the word and the universe came to life.
Teach us to use words with respect and care,
Knowing the great good and the great harm that words can do.

PRAYERS FOR CHILDREN, CHRISTOPHER HERBERT

❖

Achievements

You should now be able to:

- Employ one more skill effectively in your teaching.
- Start to develop a facility in a second skill.
- Recognize that you can achieve most things if you are prepared to take risks.

SECTION FIVE

SHARING AND CARING

UNIT A:
REACHING OUT

Aims of the unit
- To look at the importance of outreach in the local community.
- To discuss the organization of midweek and holiday clubs.
- To explore a parish's relationship with the local school.

Bible passage: Luke 10:1–11

Introduction: Always on a Sunday?

Most people automatically link worship and children's work with Sunday, but this pattern is changing fast. Nearly half of our churches have regular midweek services and, as we read in Unit 1B, 'Tell the next generation', a large number of parishes spend time and money on providing midweek and holiday clubs. With more flexible working hours, Sunday activities and greater mobility, we have to look at the whole week when planning the most effective children's work.

We have already read that Sunday Schools have spent most of their history teaching about the faith to children who did not normally go to church. If we confine our children's work to Sunday, we are probably only nurturing the children of our established congregations. This excludes outreach to other children at a time when most of them will learn very little about what it means to be a Christian from their schools or their families.

When we look at the Gospels and the Acts of the Apostles, we read about Jesus and the apostles teaching in the synagogue, but we read far more about them teaching in the streets, the countryside and in people's homes. They met people where they were. We need to do the same for our children.

The most common forms of outreach are:

- Family Services
- Baptismal follow-up
- Parent and toddler clubs
- Pre-school groups
- Involvement in the local school
- Activity days
- Holiday clubs
- Midweek clubs
- Uniformed organizations
- Choir, bell-ringers, and other specialized interests
- Special youth worship

Think or discuss

1. Take a wide piece of paper. Divide it into four columns. Head them: Church group, Church links, No connection, Not happening.
2. Using the above list, make a profile of your church's outreach to children by putting each item into one of the columns. Add any other children's activities that happen in your community.
3. Look at the first three columns in turn. Think or discuss whether or not your church activities are going well. Consider how your church could strengthen links or make initial contact with non-church groups.
4. Now look at the fourth column. Is there a glaring gap, such as no family or youth worship, or nothing for young children and their families? This may be because there is little demand or the personnel are not available, but it may be because nobody has thought about it.

A model profile is at the end of this unit. Whatever needs and opportunities for outreach you have noted, do not feel that you personally have to do them or, indeed, that some-body has to address them all. The big question is, 'How do we prioritize the opportunities that we have for outreach?' That is a matter for your church council or mission committee to debate, though you may be the one to raise the subject. In this unit, we will discuss two major forms of reaching children, through church-led clubs and through contact with schools.

Planning a fun morning, holiday or midweek club

- The basic plans are the same for an activity morning or a regular club.
- Use people and organizations to help you. Your diocesan or denominational children's adviser and various Christian organizations should provide resources and training. This will include advice on health and safety matters. You will find further information in Appendix C.
- If this is your first club, invite your children's adviser or an experienced leader from another church to help you with your planning. Use a published resource as the basis of your programme. There are several examples listed in Appendix B.
- You need to register your activity with the Social Services if it involves care of children under 8 years for two hours or more a day on six or more occasions during the year. Contact your local office for further help. It is a good idea to tell your local Out of School officer about your club anyway as he or she may be able to offer practical help or know of children who would benefit from it.
- Gear your programme to the number of leaders available, the premises and facilities.
- Decide on the age range of your membership. It is not advisable to have children under 5 years in the same activities as older children.
- Insist on prior booking and make a small charge. This helps with preparation, guarantees an income and is a way of ensuring that the children value the club. In cases of hardship, it is easy to offer membership at a reduced rate. Grants are sometimes available from charities and the local authorities.
- Start slowly and gently with small numbers. Extend the work when you are ready. A common danger is to overstretch your resources at the beginning in a rush of enthusiasm.

Schools

Part of our outreach has to be by our finding ways of being the Church in the community rather than waiting or even encouraging people to come to us. A Christian presence should also be a Christian witness. Given that a school is a community where representatives of several hundred people of all ages and backgrounds meet under one roof, it is well worth while forging links with the local school.

Basic information

Entry to any school at any time is by the Head's invitation only. That applies to school governors, parents and clergy as much as other visitors.

You need the Head's or maybe the governors' permission to distribute publicity or information about activities or clubs.

If you have direct contact with the children, for example as a classroom assistant, you will have to be police checked. This is a simple procedure but it may be several weeks before you receive the result.

You must not proselytize. Your aim should be to inform and familiarize the children with the Christian faith and the way that Christians practise it, not to make converts.

Most schools are friendly places that welcome helpers. Teachers, however, are often overworked and hard-pressed. For your own sake as well as the children's, guard against being used as if you were a member of staff. Always insist on attending meetings and being briefed before an activity, and never be with the children without a teacher present.

Assisting with acts of worship or Religious Education

State schools fall into three categories: Church Aided, Church Controlled and Community schools. The status of the school affects the acts of worship and Religious Education that take place. It is vital to know this before becoming involved in acts of worship or any RE teaching. Study the following table before considering working in any school.

	Church Aided	Church Controlled	Community
Governing body	Church has majority of places on governing body.	Church has minority of places on governing body.	No formal Church representation on governing body.
Acts of worship	According to the religious denomination.	According to the religious denomination.	Majority of acts of worship should be broadly Christian.
RE lessons	According to the religious denomination.	Local agreed syllabus.	Local agreed syllabus.
Church services	Parental right of withdrawal from attendance at services.	Parental right of withdrawal from attendance at services.	Parental permission required for child to attend services.

If you are invited to take part in an act of worship, find out exactly which children will be present, their ages and something about them. The best way to do this would be by attending one. This will familiarize you with the surroundings and give you some idea of the time and format required. It will also allow the children to see you, so that you are not a complete stranger.

All acts of worship have to follow a plan. The school is required to record the subject used, together with other information. The staff usually plan the acts of worship in half-term blocks. Knowing the topics and attending the planning group's meeting is advisable. Careful preparation is vital.

All Religious Education schemes of work include teaching on the signs and symbols used by different religions and places of pilgrimage. As we have already discussed in Unit 2B, 'Hidden treasures', your church building is a wonderful teaching aid. Many schools would welcome a chance to visit your church, especially if you can provide an information sheet or talk about the building. One of the most common questions is, 'Do you still have services?' Here is an opportunity to explain that your church is a living community, not just a piece of history.

Pastoral contact

School premises are ideal places for holiday or midweek clubs. Rent is usually reasonable and, in the case of a Church school, may involve little more than paying for the caretaker's services and insurance. It may also be possible to reach young mothers by running an occasional pram service in the school hall. Many parents will attend a simple service if it is in familiar surroundings, but would not feel at ease in a church.

Church schools usually welcome visitors from the church at their special acts of worship, plays and concerts.

The church can also invite the children to take part in its life by providing a stall at a fête, displaying artwork in church or by having invitations to specific services.

Paid or voluntary work

There is a shortage of school governors. People with skills in book-keeping, building, health and safety, the law and employment are especially welcome.

Schools also welcome regular help in the classroom, such as hearing children read, or people with a particular skill, like coaching a sport or playing a musical instrument. People to help with school outings are also appreciated but should already be known to the particular class or a parent of a child in it.

Bible reading

This is Luke's longest account about mission. He does not discuss the content of the teaching but concentrates on the organization and the possible results. See how the passage can relate to your outreach.

The Lord chose another 72 men and sent them out two by two, to go ahead of him to every town and place where he himself was about to go. He said to them, 'There is a large harvest, but few workers to gather it in... Go! I am sending you like lambs among wolves. Don't take a purse or a beggar's bag or shoes; don't stop to greet anyone on the road. Whenever you go into a house, first say, "Peace be with this house." If a peace-loving person lives there, let your greeting of peace remain on him; if not take back your greeting of peace. Stay in that same house, eating and drinking whatever they offer you, for workers should be given their pay. Don't move round from one house to another. Whenever you go into a town and are made welcome, eat what is set before you, heal the sick in that town, and say to the people there, "The Kingdom of God has come near you." But whenever you go into a town and are not welcomed, go out in the streets and say, "Even the dust from your town that sticks to our feet we wipe off against you. But remember that the Kingdom of God has come near you!"'

LUKE 10:1–11

Think or discuss

- Jesus sent the disciples out in pairs, to give mutual support and so that they could bear witness to each other. He enthuses them by describing the opportunities (a large harvest) but warns them about the dangers and stresses. They are a few workers sent like sheep among wolves.
- Jesus sent them ahead of him to prepare for his teaching. 'The Kingdom of God has come near you.' They are to find the places where he will be welcomed. Only then will he come to proclaim his Good News. Outreach takes time and patience.
- Jesus gave strict instructions about travelling light and about behaviour towards the people the disciples would meet on the way. The disciples take what they need but nothing that is unnecessary.
- Jesus gives equally clear instructions about the way to respond to being welcomed or shunned. In the first place, the disciples are to start work and accept help in the shape of hospitality. In the second, they are not to persist with their message but simply move on to another place. This has implications for our own work in the local community. We need to learn to work with other people or organizations. We also need to learn to recognize and set aside projects that are not going to succeed.

❖

Case study: April Fools' fun morning

St Margaret's, Lowspring, has no children's work at present. A few young families attend the monthly Family Service that the new Rector has just started. He and the Wardens invite the diocesan children's adviser to discuss with them ways of reaching out to the children of the village. Eventually they decide that they will hold an activity morning that includes some Christian teaching and will link with the family service on the next day.

- What research is needed before embarking on this programme?
- How do you suggest that they make it known to the local children?

- What would be a suitable Christian input, remembering that most of the youngsters will have no knowledge of the faith and may never have been into the church?
- How can the congregation as a whole become involved?

Administration and health and safety issues will also form part of the planning. These are vital components of any activity. They are discussed in detail in Unit 5B, 'Keeping safe'.

Further action

- If your profile of the children's work leads you to think that you should start some activity or encourage the church to start one, take time to think and pray about it.
- Research your plans by asking questions in the community, the schools, health centre and library as well as at church.
- Think about what strengths and resources the parish already has, whether it can provide financial and other support, the venue and possible people to help lead it.
- Talk to your priest or minister before taking your plans to the PCC for its approval and support.

Prayer
Lord of the Harvest,
the harvest is plentiful and the labourers are few,
but you make your Church fruitful with many ministries.
We pray for our parish,
that we may grasp the opportunities of the present time.
Father, Lord of creation, in your mercy, hear us.
PATTERNS FOR WORSHIP

❖

Achievements

You should now be able to:

- See the importance of reaching out to children within your local community.
- Sketch a profile of your local children's work and be able to discuss possible ways to develop it.
- Have the basic tools for starting to organize an activity day or holiday club.
- Understand the opportunities and challenges of the church working with its local school.

PROFILE OF THE CHILDREN'S WORK IN AND AROUND ST PETER'S, HIGHSTOW

Church Group	Church Links	No Connection	Not Happening
Quarterly Family Service	Scouts and Cubs attend Family Service	Pre-school in village	Baptismal follow-up
Parent and Toddler club meets weekly	Vicar visits county primary school	Guides and Brownies	
Fun morning each half term		Holiday club at the local Baptist church	Midweek club
Mostly youth at evening service			No choir. Bells not used

Activities to be explored

Consider having the Family Service once a month. Look at whether there are any adjustments to be made to the evening service, as the congregation is mostly youngsters.

The parent and toddler club is successful and most of the parents come to church. Perhaps there is an informal baptismal follow-up going on! The children move on to the village pre-school. That provides a Christian presence, although it is not a formal one. There would be no benefit in setting up a rival pre-school.

Although the Scouts and Cubs are not church groups, they have good relations with the church. It may be worth finding out why the Guides and Brownies do not come to the Family Service. They may attend another church, or perhaps they will respond to an invitation.

Midweek work needs development. If the activity days are successful, consider expanding one into a club lasting three mornings. Use the vicar's links with the school to invite the children to it. See that it ends with a Family Service on the Sunday. It may be possible to combine with the local Baptist church in providing a summer holiday club.

Bell-ringing could provide an activity for some of the youth club if a tutor could be found. Contact the County Association of Change Ringers for help. Alternatively, you could start a youth house-group to provide a forum for discussion and other activities.

Eighteen months later

A possible scenario about eighteen months later is that the church has established monthly Family Services. The Scouts and Cubs still attend quarterly, the Guides do not attend, but six Brownies came on Mothering Sunday.

Two of the young mothers are now on the local pre-school committee. The leaders who ran the activity days asked their diocesan children's adviser to help them plan a three-morning event. She also gave them advice on involving other members of the congregation. Every child in the local school was invited and nearly 50 children attended. Three leaders are going to help with the holiday club at the Baptist church.

There is a young people's house-group that meets fortnightly for Bible study and general discussion. It is also helping to strengthen friendships and links with the church. Members of the youth group provided a short drama for the Harvest Supper. The youngsters were not interested in bell-ringing, but the boys have started a five-a-side football team. The father of one of them, who does not normally attend church, is their coach.

UNIT B:
KEEPING SAFE

Aims of the unit
- To examine some basic rules of behaviour management.
- To address basic health and safety issues.
- To review child protection legislation and good practice.

Bible passage: Matthew 18:2–6

Introduction: Is your children's group a school, a family or a club?

'It is a bit of all of them. The children are there to learn about God, but it is not really school. I am always telling them that we are all part of God's family, and I like to think of myself as the children's friend, a person they can talk to and have fun with. We call our group the "Godbods", and we all have badges, so it is a club as well.'

So, how do you expect the children to behave? As if they were at school, at home or in their own club? How should they behave in church or Sunday club?

Many instances of bad behaviour stem from children not knowing what is expected from them. Children understand consistency. They know that when they are at school they put up their hands to answer questions, but at home they just reply. In church, the preacher asks a question and then goes on talking without expecting an answer. At school they call their teacher 'Miss Jones', but at church she becomes 'Fran'. They dash up to Mum in the playground, but they have to sit apart from her when they come into church.

Every family and community has rules. They make children feel more secure because they set out their boundaries. If the children are involved in making their own rules, then they are more likely to accept and own them. Most classrooms in your local school will have class rules that the children have agreed upon, pinned up in a prominent position. Think about doing this with your group. Start, if you wish, with the great commandments concerned with loving God and our neighbour: the way to treat God and his house, the church; the way to be kind and considerate to other people. The way that you behave towards the children will also have a big effect on their behaviour. This includes the way you organize your session.

Ten Commandments of behaviour management

1. Always see that the space you are using is prepared before the session. This helps the children to know that you are ready for them and that their session matters to you.
2. Sitting around a space like the edge of a rug or in a circle has a calming effect.
3. People speak at a higher pitch and more quickly when they are nervous or anxious. Before you start, take a minute to be alone and pray, 'Lord, I know that you are with me'. Take deep breaths and speak deliberately and calmly, even when things are going wrong.
4. Seat the children so that you can use eye contact. Wait calmly for their attention and then speak.
5. Do not say too much at once. Give one command at a time.
6. Never let chat develop, or try to talk over it. Stop it from the beginning.
7. If two youngsters misbehave, let them choose the solution: 'Would you be better sitting apart for the story, or can you stay together and manage to listen sensibly?' If this does not work, set the two culprits apart, but give them a chance to do something together later.
8. Ask questions of miscreants: 'What is our rule about going into church? ... Yes, you walk in quietly. Now show that you have remembered it.'
9. Celebrate what is good. Be generous with praise, especially when a child achieves something he or she personally finds difficult.
10. Never suggest that a child is less precious to you or to God

because of his or her behaviour. Never punish a child by preventing him from taking part in worship or by humiliating him in front of his peers. The old maxim, 'Hate the sin and love the sinner', always holds true.

Nobody is just naughty. It is always for a reason. Some of the reasons are obvious; others are deep-seated and it would not be appropriate to attempt to examine them or look for facile solutions. Getting to know the children, their families and their interests is an essential part of our work.

Sometimes you will have a child with serious behavioural or learning difficulties. Do not struggle on your own or allow this situation to dominate the group. Ask for advice from the parents and insist that you have a helper assigned to the child. If appropriate, talk separately to the child and ask what helps them to resolve the particular difficulty.

Think or discuss

- Discuss any ways in which you could improve upon your present method of leading your group.
- How are you addressing any instances of bad behaviour? Does your response demonstrate that the person still has an intrinsic value, however unacceptable the behaviour is?
- Discuss any particular difficulties and share advice. Remember that individual cases should remain confidential to the group.

Take care of your valuables

Children are one of the Church's most valuable assets. A church without children is a dying church. Children have much to offer a church and, as we discussed in Unit 3A, a church that takes its children seriously will always receive a sense of vitality and hope through them. They are also the most vulnerable part of the Christian family, so their care and nurture should be one of the most important parts of our ministry.

When we are working with children, we are *in loco parentis*, taking the place of the parents. This is too big a responsibility to rely on good will and chance. We cannot know a group of youngsters as well as parents know their own children, so we need simple procedures to help us.

Documentation

- Have a register with personal details so that, should a parent need to be contacted or a child not turn up, the data is readily accessible. Always keep it on the premises. Ask the parent to fill in a registration form to provide basic information when a child joins the group.
- Keep notes with the register about illnesses and other conditions. It is a good idea to invite information about learning difficulties, fears and family situations like a death or an absent parent as well as medical conditions.
- If your club involves children aged under 8 years for two hours or more a day on six or more occasions in a year, you need to register it with the local authority. Contact your Early Years and Childcare officers for further help. There is a nationwide initiative to develop Out of School projects and work with Early Years, so it is advisable to register your club anyway. Advantages may include publicity, inspection, training and funding.

Personnel

- Leaders should have experience of looking after or working with young people if they are to take charge of any group or activity. Those who have not can gain it by helping an experienced leader. Youngsters aged less than 18 years are often valuable and capable helpers but should not work without an adult.
- If adults or teenage helpers are to be working with children regularly, they should undertake training. Studying this book should give you a lot of the basic information that you need and it can be used as the basis of a formal training course. Your diocese, denomination and various Christian organizations will advise you of other training courses being held in your area.
- Always take great care when involving an adult who is not well known to the children. See that your church council endorses every new leader or helper before he or she starts working with a group.

- Every denomination has its child protection guidelines. These stipulate that every new leader should offer references, which must be taken up, and fill in a criminal declaration form. If a person is unwilling to sign such a form or you are uneasy about their suitability, do not use them. It is better to risk offending an adult than harming a child.
- The Home Office Guidelines, *Safe from Harm*, recommend a minimum ratio of one adult to every eight children aged 8 years. There should be more adults if the children are younger or if they are having an activity away from the premises.
- The numbers of leaders available, the size of the premises and standard of facilities form the basis of the programme that you can run. Never be tempted to take extra children or to go outside your planned age range. It is not advisable to have children under 5 years in the same activities as older children unless there is a special area for younger children or parents and helpers sitting in with toddlers.

Outings
- Send details to parents of any activity taking place away from the usual meeting place, with a consent form that includes permission for medical treatment to be given in an emergency. Always keep consent forms with you.
- All applicants should fill in consent and health forms for events like holiday clubs and fun mornings.
- Check with the church's insurance company that you are covered for activities that take place away from the church premises.
- If you use private cars for an outing, inform the parents of the names of the drivers. You should also check the drivers' insurance and licences. Never overload a car or travel in one that does not have suitable seatbelts.

Safety
- The premises should be safe and well maintained. If the club meets frequently, have an occasional fire drill. See that leaders know how to evacuate the building quickly or get help in emergency.
- Have a properly stocked first aid kit with one assigned person, preferably trained, to take charge of all first aid.

- Do not let young children go home without an adult unless the parent has specifically said that they may do so. Never let a child go with another adult unless the parent has informed you that this will be happening.
- Never let children go off the premises without permission or singly. In large youth groups, the best procedure is to have a signing-out book.
- With large groups, have some simple safety rules such as lining up for drinks, asking before going to the toilet, standing still when the whistle blows. This will lower the risk of accidents as well as improving the quality of the activities.

Think or discuss
- Using the above checklist as a guide, walk around the church premises to check for health and safety matters.
- Look at any documentation concerned with children's work.
- Note items or procedures that are not in place and resolve to improve them or alert the person responsible.
- If you are not at your own church, do this in your imagination and check any queries when you are next there.

Child protection
Since the introduction of the Children Act in 1989, the care and welfare of children has come on to the agenda of every organization that has contact with them. This has coincided with media publicity about long-standing cases of child abuse, some being in Christian organizations. Every diocese and denomination has a child protection policy, which your church should follow. Most of the policy is concerned with good practice and common sense.

When something is wrong
It is possible that at some time you will be in contact with a child who is suffering from inappropriate behaviour or child abuse. This occurs in families of all backgrounds and cultures. It takes four forms: physical, emotional, sexual or neglect. If you notice something that concerns you

or a child confides in you, it is vital that you take it seriously and follow correct procedures. You can find these in your child protection policy. If you are doubtful what to do, do not ask your friends or set the matter aside, but contact your denominational child protection officer, the NSPCC Helpline or local Social Services and ask for an informal discussion. You will find further information about this in Appendix C.

See that you and your fellow leaders and clergy have training in child protection. Local Authorities and Christian organizations hold regular courses.

The last thought

Lastly, the Church is a home for sinners like you and me. It is also a haven for criminals who prey on children. It is our duty to exercise a ministry of forgiveness but it is also our duty to protect the vulnerable from harm. Good practice combined with active interest in the children's work from the church council reduces risk of injury or abuse to its lowest level. It allows us to feel confident that our children are kept safe and happy, receive high-quality nurture and are given opportunities to grow in faith as children of God.

Bible reading

This passage is about status, and people who were new to the faith rather than specifically about children, but we can use it literally when thinking about our attitude to the young people in our care.

Jesus called a child, made him stand in front of them, and said, 'I assure you that unless you change and become like children, you will never enter the Kingdom of heaven. The greatest in the Kingdom of heaven is the one who humbles himself and becomes like this child. And whoever welcomes in my name one such child as this, welcomes me.

'If anyone should cause one of these little ones to lose his faith in me, it would be better for that person to have a large millstone tied round his neck and be drowned in the deep sea.'

MATTHEW 18:2–6

❖

Think or discuss

- 'Whoever welcomes in my name one such child as this, welcomes me.' How do we really welcome children?
- Are we reconcilers when the needs of young and old apparently conflict?
- 'If anyone should cause one of these little ones to lose his faith in me, it would be better for that person to have a large millstone tied round his neck and be drowned in the deep sea.' Have any decisions made by your church during the last year discouraged children and young families from coming to church?
- Is your church a place where children feel safe and valued?

Case study: I am angry!

Kevin is aged 12. He attends the Sunday evening youth group regularly, but is often disruptive. He fidgets, kicks chairs and makes sarcastic remarks about the teaching and the various activities. The leaders have admitted to each other that they are relieved when he does not turn up. One evening, they have been discussing prayer. Suddenly Kevin explodes, 'It is all a lot of rubbish. One day when I was all alone and things were bad, I asked God to send someone to come to help me, but nobody came!'

- The leader's response was, 'Well, I am here now and I am listening.' Do you think that was a good reply?
- How would you have continued your conversation with Kevin after that reply?
- It is clear that Kevin is very angry about something. What is the best way to help him to come to terms with the things that are causing his anger?
- What place do listening and reassurance have in your time with Kevin? How would you conclude the conversation?
- Remember that should a child's confidences include alleged abuse or neglect, you must take it seriously and report it to the authorities.

❖

Further action

- Review your behaviour management policy. See that it is consistent and fair.
- Familiarize yourself with your child protection guidelines if you have not done so already.
- Note the telephone numbers of the NSPCC, Childline and local Social Services.

The first unit of this book stressed that the priest or minister and the church council have the ultimate legal responsibility for the children's work. Do they take this responsibility seriously? Speak to them if you have concerns that cannot be easily resolved.

❖

Prayer

O God,
You are filled with tender love
For those who live in fear.
Bless all children who live in fear;
afraid of someone at home;
afraid of someone at school;
afraid of a relation;
afraid of someone who has treated them wrongly.
Give all those children the wisdom
they need to know whom they can trust,
so that their fears can be heard,
and justice and truth prevail.
And then bring to their wounded minds and souls
the healing of your peace.

CHRISTOPHER HERBERT, PRAYERS FOR CHILDREN

❖

Achievements

You should now be able to:

- Understand and use good practice in behaviour management.
- See the importance of knowing your children as individuals.
- Follow basic health and safety and child protection procedures.
- Be able to discern when you need advice or help and how to get it.

POSTSCRIPT:
THE NEXT STEP

As we have already agreed, reading a book about children's work or even discussing it in a group is not the only way or even the best way to retain knowledge. You will need to 'earth' it by putting into practice the things that you have learned over the last few weeks. You will learn from the children, and from your other leaders. When things go well, be glad and remember what happened. When you have had a bad session, look calmly at what went wrong and learn from it.

Leaders and helpers learn from looking back at a term's activities and evaluating them. They learn from meeting to discuss the work, swapping ideas and information, and from encouraging each other. This book may have given you enough help for the present. You may want to study further. Your denomination or diocese should be able to point you in the direction of further training.

However, that is all about giving out. We also need to let our faith grow and to spend time in prayer and study of the scriptures if we are to be effective Christian leaders and teachers. This means giving adequate time to be with God and with other people. Are there things that you need to modify or even give up in order to allow this to happen?

Bible reading

Being fired up for children's work brings its own rewards. It also can bring the tiredness and lack of energy commonly called 'burn out'. In the following passage, Jesus recognizes the need for his disciples to take time to sit at his feet, if the flame of their ministries is to continue to burn brightly.

> Jesus and his disciples came to a village where a woman named
> Martha welcomed him in her home. She had a sister named

Mary, who sat down at the feet of the Lord and listened to his teaching. Martha was upset over all the work she had to do, so she came and said, 'Lord, don't you care that my sister has left me to do all the work by myself? Tell her to come and help me!'

The Lord answered her, 'Martha, Martha! You are worried and troubled over so many things, but just one is needed. Mary has chosen the right thing, and it will not be taken away from her.'

LUKE 10:38–42

Think or discuss

- As children's leaders, we are very good Marthas. We are warm and welcoming. We rush around and organize everything. We often feel isolated and get annoyed.
- As children's leaders, we also need to be like Mary, to stop every so often and enjoy being with God. We need time to explore our faith. Then our children will copy us and learn how to hear and respond when Jesus says, 'Follow me.'
- However much we enjoy our work with children, we all need to have time to step back from the work and take a complete break. This can be by working on a rota or by asking a former leader to take over for a few weeks. Another kind of rest is by the children's leaders having an occasional meal or outing together, just to enjoy each other's company.
- When a situation changes in our personal or church life, we need to be able to discern whether it is right for us to continue as we are or to modify our role in children's work. We also need to be prepared to consider moving on to another ministry when the time is right.

The aim of this book is to give children's leaders some of the tools needed to produce effective children's work. These include prayer, Bible study and worship, as much as teaching and learning skills. They also include knowing how children develop as whole people and how to keep them safe as valued members of the Christian family. This is a responsible and daunting task, but one of the most important ministries in the Church.

Prayer

Take, Lord, and receive all my liberty,
my memory, my understanding and my entire will,
all that I have and possess.

You have given all to me,
to you, Lord, I return it.

All is yours;
do with it what you will.

Give me only your love and your grace,
that is enough for me.
IGNATIUS LOYOLA (1491–1556)

APPENDIX A

Suggested programme for a condensed course

The following course will last for five sessions, each of approximately 90 minutes, plus a practical workshop. It covers about 65 per cent of the work in the book, the rest being read individually by the participants. Unless stated otherwise, every session is divided into three parts, each lasting about 30 minutes.

First Session: Section 1, Units A and B

1. Start with the introduction, 'Making Christ known'. Invite each person to introduce himself or herself and say why they are doing children's work. Follow this with the Bible reading, 1 Corinthians 12:27–28. Discuss one of the questions: 'What gifts and experience can I bring to this work?'

2. Move on to 'Responsibilities and relationships'. Note that the legal responsibility for the children's work rests with the church council and that it should support its children's workers. Invite the group to note any of the suggestions that their church is not carrying out. Reinforce this by moving on to the case study in Section 1 Unit B, 'Why are you out there?'

3. Work through the 'Aims of children's work' exercise.

4. Close with the Bible passage, Psalm 78:1–7, and the prayer of Teresa of Avila.

Second Session: Section 2, Units A and B

1. Start with 'Come and see' and then work through the 'Use your senses' exercise. Discuss briefly the importance of using your space effectively.

2. Read the Bible passage, John 13:4–9, 12–14, and discuss the questions following it. Then discuss the case study, 'Starting and stopping'.

3. 'Let the building speak.' Spend a few minutes walking around the church looking for signs and symbols. Follow it with 'What shall

we do today?' and the brainstorming exercise.
4. Close with the prayer, 'Let all the world in every corner sing, my God and King!'

Third Session: Section 3, Units A and B

1. Start with 'Setting the scene'. Refer back to the importance of using space effectively. Work on the paragraphs on prayer and the following activity for about 20 minutes. Use the case study, 'Angela's class assemblies' if time permits it.
2. 'We welcome you into the Lord's family.' Invite the group to treat this as a checklist and spend a few minutes working individually on discussion points 1 and 2.
3. Allow an hour to work on all of Unit B, 'Growing faith'.

Fourth Session: Section 4, Unit A and part of Unit B

1. Work through the sections 'God's storybook' and 'Telling stories', with the discussion points.
2. Having looked at the checklist of 'Storytelling techniques', work in twos or threes. Read a short Bible story to each other, trying to use the suggested techniques. Move on to the drama activity in Unit B and try telling one of the suggested Bible stories as if you were there. Continue until about 15 minutes before the end of the session.
3. Use about ten minutes discussing the points at the beginning of Unit B, 'Media to help with storytelling'. Use the results as the basis for planning your practical workshop.
4. As you have spent the whole session on the Bible, finish by sitting quietly and listening to one person reading the Bible passage, Mark 4:30–33, and saying the prayer at the end of Unit A.

Fifth Session: Workshop on subjects in Section 4, Unit B

You may not want to have this workshop immediately after the fourth session. You will need time to arrange equipment or invite specialist leaders, or for members of the group to prepare a workshop on a particular interest or skill. Try to have a longer session than is usual, a long evening with a break for refreshment or, if possible, a full morning or afternoon.

You can have two workshops, each being an hour long. If you have the leaders and space, you could have three workshops, with the participants choosing two of them. See that as many people's requests are met as is possible.

If the group comes together at the end, it could review the case study, 'Friday night panic!' from Unit A or devise a short act of worship based on the reading from Unit B, Psalm 136:1–9, 26.

Sixth Session: Section 5, Units A and B, and the Postscript

1. Spend the first half hour noting the common forms of outreach in 'Always on a Sunday?' and devising a profile of your church and its links with the wider community.

2. Discuss briefly either running a weekday club or working in school according to the group's particular interests. Consolidate the work by discussing the Bible reading, Luke 10:1–11, as a strategy for outreach.

3. Spend the last block of time working on the behaviour management and child protection issues in Unit B. Remind the group that this section underpins all the other work because it is about valuing children.

4. Finish with the reading from Unit B, Matthew 18:2–6, and the prayer from Unit A, 'Lord of the Harvest'. If the group comes from several churches and will not meet again, consider using the reading and prayer from the Postscript instead.

Appendix B

Further reading

Section 1: Called to communicate

Unit A: What do I have to offer?
Become Like a Child, Kathryn Copsey (SU, 1994)
Children in the Church? B. Pedley and J. Muir (NS/CHP, 1997)
Help! There's a Child in My Church, Peter Graystone (SU, 1989)
Seen and Heard, Jackie Cray (Monarch, 1995)

Unit B: Tell the next generation
God, Kids and Us: The growing edge of ministry with children, Eibner and Walker (Morehouse, 1997)
Offering the Gospel to Children, G. Wolff Pritchard (Cowley, 1992)
The Rise and Role of the Sunday School Movement, P. Cliff (NCEC, 1986)
Unfinished Business (Children and the Churches), CGMC (CCBI, 1995)

Section 2: Using our senses

Unit A: Do you understand?
Godly Play, Jerome W. Berryman (Augsburg, 1991)
How Children Learn, J. Holt (Penguin, 1983)
Sharing Jesus with Under Fives, Janet Gaukroger (Crossway, 1994)
Teaching Godly Play, Jerome W. Berryman (Abingdon Press, 1995)
The Contours of Christian Education, Ed. J. Asley and D. Day (McCrimmons, 1992)

Unit B: Hidden treasures
Advent Angels, Sue Doggett (BRF, 1998)
Feast of Faith, K. and S. Parkes (NS/CHP, 2000)
Festive Allsorts, Nicola Currie (NS/CHP, 1993)
My Book of Special Times of Year et al., Anne Faulkner (BRF, 1999)

Talking Together: The Christian Year with under fives, Patricia Beall Gavigan (Cassell, 1996)
The Easter Garden et al., Jenny Hyson (BRF, 1996)

Section 3: Worship and spirituality

Unit A: An encounter with the living God
Celebration! Celebrating for all God's Family, M. Withers and T. Pinchin (Gracewing, 1995)
Lion Book of First Prayers, Su Box (Lion, 1998)
Prayers for Children, Christopher Herbert (NS/CHP, 1995)
The 'E' Book, Gill Ambrose (NS/CHP, 2000)
Worship through the Christian Year, eds. D. Murrie and H. Bruce (NS/CHP, 1998)

Unit B: Growing faith
Caring for the Whole Child, John Bradford (Children's Society, 1995)
Children Finding Faith, Francis Bridger (SU, 2000)
Christian Perspectives on Faith Development, J. Astley and L. Francis (Gracewing, 1994)
Don't Just Do Something—Sit There, Mary K. Stone (RMEP, 1995)
How Faith Grows, Jeff Astley (NS/CHP, 1991)
Looking Beyond, Jill Fuller (Kevin Mayhew, 1996)
The Spirit of the Child, D. Hay and R. Nye (HarperCollins, 1998)

Section 4: The place of story

Unit A: The word of the Lord
On the Story Mat et al., Brian Ogden (BRF, 1998)
Just Time to Catch the Post et al., Brian Ogden (BRF, 1999)
Special Days at Daisy Hill School, Brian Ogden (BRF, 1999)
Downs and Ups at Daisy Hill School, Brian Ogden (BRF, 1999)
Children's Guide to the Bible, R. Willoughby (SU, 1998)
In God's Name et al., Sandy Eisenberg Sasso (Deep Books, 1994)
Lion Children's Bible, Pat Alexander (Lion, 1991)

Beginning with God et al., Rachel Heathfield (BRF, 2000)
Tell It Again, Michele Taylor (NCEC, 2000)
The Bible: A Children's Playground, R. and G. Gobbel (SCM, 1986)
Toby & Trish and the Amazing Book of Acts et al., Margaret Withers (BRF, 1999)
Using the Bible with Children, Rosemary Cox (Grove Books, 2000)

Unit B: Mime, music and movement
Acting Up: Plays on the Word, Derek Haylock (NS/CHP, 1999)
Another 100+ Ideas for Drama, Anna Scher & Charles Verrall (Heinemann, 1989)
Easy Ways to Christmas Plays et al., Vicki Howie (BRF, 1997)
Jesus and Peter, John L. Bell and Graham Maule (Wild Goose, 1999)
The Dramatised Bible, ed. Michael Perry (HarperCollins, 1989)

A Year of Celebration, ed. J. Porter and J. McCrimmon (McCrimmons, 1995)
Big Blue Planet, ed. Judy Jarvis (Stainer & Bell, 1998)
Junior Praise, ed. P. Horrobin and G. Leavers (Marshall Pickering, 1990)
Kidsource, Alan Price (Mayhew, 1999)
The Complete Come and Praise, Geoffrey Marshall-Taylor (BBC, 1988)

Heaven in a Poem, Lois Rock (Lion, 2000)
Let's Join In! Christine Wright (SU, 1990)
Poems and Prayers for a Better World, Su Box (Lion, 2000)
Whispering in God's Ear, Alan MacDonald (Lion, 1998)

Hand and Glove Puppets, Judith Simmons (LPP, 1995)
Puppets in Service (Scripts: Six volumes), Harry Barrett (One Way UK, 1999)
Solo Puppeteering, Harry Barrett (One Way UK, 1998)

All Age Events and Worship, Tony Castle (HarperCollins, 1994)
Footprints in Faith, Katie Thompson (Kevin Mayhew, 1999)
Liturgical Posters, Turvey Abbey (St Paul Media Centres)

Section 5: Sharing and caring

Unit A: Reaching out
Building New Bridges, Claire Gibb (NS/CHP, 1996)
Go for Gold (book and video) et al., Ron Fountain (SU, 2000)
Easy Ways to Bible Fun for the Very Young, Vicki Howie (BRF, 2001)
Plagues & Promises, Gill Ambrose (NCEC, 1998)
Reaching Children, Paul Butler (SU, 1993)
The Paintbox Project et al., Elizabeth Bruce and Judy Jarvis (NCEC, 2000)

Unit B: Keeping safe
Children and Bereavement, Wendy Duffy (NS/CHP, 1995)
Children and Divorce, R. Smith and J. Bradford (NS/CHP, 1997)
Guidelines on Good Practice and Child Protection (Denominational or diocesan materials)
Safe from Harm, Home Office (HMSO, 1994)

Appendix C

Useful contacts

General advice and training

Every diocese and denomination should have a specialist children's adviser. He or she will provide information about all matters connected with children's work, visit churches and provide consultations and training for clergy and children's leaders. This service will generally be free of charge. Some dioceses also provide resources and a mailing. Contact via your diocesan or denominational office.

Other Christian organizations offer publications and training connected with children's work. Some organizations have regional field workers who will provide individual advice and support to parishes. You should find their names in your diocesan or denominational directory or obtain them from the organization's national office.

BRF
First Floor
Elsfield Hall
15–17 Elsfield Way
Oxford
OX2 8FG
01865 319700
information@brf.org.uk

Children Worldwide
Dalesdown
Honeybridge Lane
Dial Post
Horsham
West Sussex
RH13 8NZ
01403 7101712

Church Mission Society (CMS)
Partnership House
157 Waterloo Road
London
SE1 8XA
020 7928 8681
enquiries@cms-uk.org

Church Pastoral Aid Society (CPAS)
Athena Drive
Tachbrook Park
Warwick
CV34 6NG
01926 334242
mail@cpas.org.uk

National Christian Education Council (NCEC)
1020 Bristol Road
Selly Oak
Birmingham
B29 6LB
0121 472 4242
ncec@network.co.uk

One Way UK Creative Ministries
(Interdenominational)
Tyndale Baptist Church
2–4 Cressingham Road
Reading
RG2 7JE
0118 975 6303
info@onewayuk.com

PCCA Christian Child Care
PO Box 133
Swanley
Kent
BR8 7UQ
01322 667207
Helpline 01322 660011
info@pcca.co.uk

Royal School of Church Music
Cleveland Lodge
Westhumble
Dorking
Surrey
RH5 6BW
01306 877676
cl@rscm.com

Rural Sunrise (Sunrise Ministries)
2 The Old Forge
Gardner Street
Herstmonceux
Hailsham
East Sussex
BN27 4LE
01323 832083

Scripture Union
207-209 Queensway
Bletchley
Milton Keynes
Buckinghamshire
MK2 2EB
01908 856000
info@scriptureunion.org.uk

Christian charities offering publications for use in children's work

Children's Society
Edward Rudolf House
Margery Street
London
WC1X 0JL
020 7841 4400
hq-reception@the-childrens-society.org.uk

Christian Aid
PO Box 100
London
SE1 7RT
020 7620 4444
caid@gn.apc.org

Crosslinks
251 Lewisham Way
London
SE4 1XF
020 8691 6111
crosslinks@pro-net.co.uk

Mission to Seafarers
St Michael Paternoster Royal
College Hill
London
EC4R 2RL
020 7248 5202
general@missiontoseafarers.org

Mothers' Union
Mary Sumner House
24 Tufton Street
London
SW1P 3RB
020 7222 5533
mu@themothersunion.org

United Society for the Propagation of the
Gospel (USPG)
Partnership House
157 Waterloo Road
London
SE1 8XA
020 7928 8681
enquiries@uspg.org.uk

Health and safety

First Aid courses are available through your local Early Years or Childcare Partnership and St John Ambulance or Red Cross. Contact your local area offices. Staff will also give advice on the suitability of premises and maximum numbers of children or adults advisable for various activities.

Child protection

Every diocese and denomination has a child protection policy. You should familiarize yourself with the document and see that your church supports it. For further advice, contact your diocesan or denominational office.

PCCA Christian Child Care provides an advisory service, training, publications and a 24-hour helpline. It also advises on fostering and adoption issues, and provides counselling for issues of past abuse.

The NSPCC has a 24-hour helpline. Call it on 0800 800500. It also has local child protection teams. They are listed in the phone book.

If you are concerned about a child or need to discuss a matter concerning child abuse, contact your denominational child protection officer, the NSPCC or PCCA. You may also contact Social Services or the police and ask if you can have an informal discussion with the duty officer connected with child abuse. You will not have to give your name or the name of the child. Contact numbers will be in your local telephone directory.

INDEX OF SUBJECTS